Art of
ENGLISH CONVERSATION

Speak English Fluently

Published by
Lotus Press Publishers & Distributors

Art of ENGLISH CONVERSATION

Speak English Fluently

Deepa Verma

Lotus PRESS
4735/22, Prakash Deep Building,
Ansari Road, Daryaganj,
New Delhi- 110002

Lotus Press : Publishers & Distributors
Unit No. 220, 2nd Floor, 4735/22, Prakash Deep Building,
Ansari Road, Darya Ganj, New Delhi- 110002
Ph. 41325510, 98118-38000
• E-mail : lotuspress1984@gmail.com
www.lotuspress.co.in

Art of English Conversation

ISBN: 978-81-8382-259-6

Printed & Published by : **Lotus Press Publishers & Distributors,** New Delhi-02

PREFACE

Four skills are required while learning a language – listening, speaking, reading and writing. Out of these, the skill of speaking is different and is also one of the most important as well. The other three you can do alone, on your own, without anyone else. You can listen to the radio alone. You can read a book alone. You can write a letter alone. But you can't really speak alone! For practicing the skill of speaking fluently, you need to have a partner who is well conversant in the language and who would encourage you to speak your mind without any hitches. It is also important that people whom you converse with don't make you feel inferior when it comes to conversing freely.

That is why you should make every effort possible to find somebody to speak with. Find people who can speak English with you. At school, you should use the opportunity to speak to your teachers and other students. If your teacher asks you a question, take the opportunity to answer. Try to say as much as possible. If your teacher asks you to speak in pairs or groups with other students, try to say as much as possible. Don't worry about your mistakes. Just speak!

Many cities around the world have conversation clubs where people can exchange one language for another. Try to find a conversation club near you.

If you are living in an English-speaking country, you have a wonderful opportunity. Practice speaking to the local people such as shop owners or taxi drivers. Even if you don't live in an English-speaking country, there are often restaurants in many large cities. If you can find one of these, you'll probably meet many people speaking English as a first or second language.

Everywhere you go you find language. Shop names, street names, advertisements, notices on buses and trains... Even if you are not in an English-speaking country, there are often a lot of English words you can see. When walking down the street, practice reading the words and numbers that you see. Say them to yourself. It's not exactly a conversation, but it will help you to 'think' in English.

Don't be afraid to speak. You must try to speak, even if you make mistakes. You cannot learn without mistakes. The present book is to help you improve English conversation. Hope it proves to be of great help.

Author

CONTENTS

1. English Conversation 11

What is English Conversation? 11

Learning Basic English Conversation with a Tutor 12

Mastering the Art of Conversation 13

- General Tips 15
- Error Correction Tips 15
- Grammar Tips 16
- Vocabulary Tips 16
- Pronunciation 16

How to Have a Great Conversation? 16

How to come up with Good Conversation Topics? 20

How to Have a Witty Conversation? 24

How to Start a Conversation when you have nothing to talk about? 27

How to Join a Conversation? 34

How to make the Conversation Flow? 36

How to Start an Interesting Conversation? 37

2. Ways to Improve English Conversation 39

Sample Dialogue in English 62

3. Strategies for English Conversation 64

How to Improve your English? 64

How to Improve your Pronunciation? 65

Taking Tests 67

Improving Vocabulary 68

Intonation and Stress 70

Differences between American and British English 72

- Use of the Present Perfect 72
- Possession 73
- The Verb Get 74
- Vocabulary 74
- Prepositions 75

- Past Simple/Past Participles 75
- Spelling 76

4. Small Talks 77

First Name, Last Name or Title? 77
- Talking TO People 77
- First Name Only 77

Title and Last Name 78
- Talking ABOUT People 78
- First Name Only 78
- Last Name Only 79
- First and Last Name 79

Introductions – Social Language 79
- Greetings – Social Language 80
- Special Days – Social Language 81
- Speaking to Strangers – Social Language 82
- Travel Greetings – Social Language 83

Starting a Conversation – Top Ten Questions 84
- Offering Help 86
- More English Functions 87

Making Small Talk 88
- What is small talk? 88
- Why is small talk difficult for some English learners? 88
- How to Improve Small Talk Skills? 88

Demanding Explanations 90

Using Vague Expressions – Being Imprecise 91
- More English Functions 92
- Formula Form 92

Asking for Information 93

Apologising in English 93

Asking for Things 94

Asking People to Repeat 95

Expressing Sympathy 96

Getting People's Attention 97

Going to Bed / Getting Up 98

Making Invitations 99

Offering Something 100

Accepting Offers 101

Phrases used at Meals 101

Phrases used when Drinking 102

Asking Polite Questions 103

5. Commonly Used Words 106

Top Most Uses of Nouns 119

Commonly Used Adjectives 124
Commonly Used Verbs, Prepositions, Articles, Pronouns, etc. 126
Commonly Used General Nouns 128
Commonly Used Specific Nouns 133

6. Improving Vocabulary 136

Confusing Words 136
Tongue Twister 141
Tongue Twisters to Practice Elocution 143
Idioms and Expressions 144
- Idioms and Expressions with Specific Words 144
- Idioms and Expressions - 'As ... As' 145

Idioms and Expressions with Verbs 149
Idioms and Expressions by Theme 154
- English Clothing Idioms 154
- English Body Idioms 156
- English Animal Idioms 159

English Idioms Featuring Animals 162

7. Improving Grammar 164

Uses of the Verb To Have 164
- To Have – Main Verb 164
- Have Got 164
- To Have – Main Verb 165
- To Have – Auxiliary Verb 165
- To Have To Do – Modal Form 166

English Prepositions 167
- One Word Prepositions 167
- Two Word Prepositions 168
- Three Word Prepositions 168

Adjective Placement 169
Verb Formation Chart 170
Passive Voice 174
- Passive Voice Structure 174

Transitive and Intransitive Verbs 175
- Transitive Verbs 175
- Intransitive Verbs 175
- Transitive AND Intransitive 176

Possessive Nouns and Possessive Adjectives 176
- Possessive Adjectives 176
- Possessive Nouns 177
- Possessive Pronouns 178

Intensifying Adjectives 179
- Absolute / Complete / Total / Utter 179

- Big 180
- Great 181
- Large 181
- Heavy 182
- High – Low. 182
- Strong 183

Defining and Non-Defining Relative Clauses 183
Deciding whether a Clause is Defining Or Non-Defining 184
- Defining Relative Clauses 184
- Non-defining Relative Clauses 184

Relative Clauses and Prepositions 187
- Defining Relative Clauses 187
- Non-Defining Relative Clauses 188

Reflexive Pronouns in English 188
- English Reflexive Pronouns 188
- Problem Areas 189

Differences between Action and Stative Verbs 190
- Action Verbs 190
- Stative Verbs 190
- Common Stative Verbs 191

Guide to Future with Will and Going to 192
- The Basics: Future with Will: 192
- The Basics: Future with Going to: 193
- Future with Will Structure: 193
- Future with Going to Structure: 193

Guide to Past Simple and Past Continuous 194
- The Basics: Simple Past: 194
- The Basics: Past Continuous: 194
- Past Simple Structure: 194
- Past Continuous Structure: 195

Passive Voice 195
- Passive Voice Structure 196

8. Common Mistakes 197

Difference between OF and FROM in English 199
- OF 199
- FROM 200

9. Exercise your Brain 211

Exercise 1 211
Exercise 2 213
Exercise 3 214
Exercise 4 216
Exercise 5 218
Exercise 6 220

CHAPTER 1

English Conversation

What is English Conversation?

Learning a new language is one of the most important skills that a person can try to master. This is true for both business and personal needs, in many cases. It's all well and good to travel to a foreign country without speaking the language, but life will be much easier and you can make new contacts far more effectively with the ability to converse. In a global business community, many are now turning to online spoken English training as a way to advance themselves on both this personal and professional level. It's no longer necessary to go to a costly language institute to gain these skills, which has opened up the world of ESL to a whole new group of people.

Conversational English is an entirely different concept than written or business English, which is what many people are taught in school. The key to success with any foreign language training; be it spoken or written, is practice, which is why many people have shied away from distance learning courses in the past. These may have just focused on long lists of vocabulary without the possibility of putting it into practice in a real setting. However, the advancements in online spoken English training now make this possible. These new advancements to the distance learning programmes include an emphasis on actually speaking, via programmes like Skype with personal tutors.

However, not everyone can afford online courses. So, here's another way to improve your conversational skills. Start off with your friends. Practicing your language skills with classmates is often a good start. Speak in English whenever you get a chance. Tell people around you to support you in the task. Instead of making fun of the mistakes, ask them to help you correct them.

Join decent chat clubs and take part in video chats. Order food from fast food joints in English. When dialing a helpline for any product or service, choose English as the language of communication.

Learning Basic English Conversation with a Tutor

Learning basic English conversation doesn't have to be a confusing experience. Learning the basics of a new language can sometimes feel intimidating. However, there are many options available for learning basic English, and many are free. English language students often find English to be a difficult language to learn because of its many grammatical rules — and exceptions to those rules — and homonyms. That's why it's extremely important to work with a native English speaker, either in person or online. A native English speaker can help you learn correct pronunciation and sentence structure so you can carry on basic conversations with ease.

Difficulty: Moderately Challenging Instructions

- Practice English with a native English speaker. Arrange your lessons so that half of the conversation is in English, and the other half is in the non-English speaker's language. Also known as conversation exchanges, this approach offers a low-key opportunity to start practicing basic conversational English immediately. Ask a family member, friend or co-worker to help you, and meet as often as both schedules allow.
- Attend free classes in your community. Many places of worship, libraries and community centres offer English classes at no

charge. The classes can range from beginner to advanced. Students may have to purchase their own texts or workbooks for the class. The style of the class may vary, with either an emphasis on speaking English only during instruction or using a combination of English and the native language of the majority of the students.

- Watch TV and listen to the radio in English. While it may be difficult in the beginning to understand what's being said, it's helpful to constantly listen to English. Many channels have a subtitle option. Read along in English while you're watching. Listening to slow-tempo songs in English can also help the English language student learn new words.
- Watch videos online. There are free English instruction videos for beginners on a number of websites. Follow along and repeat the phrases that are spoken (they may be spelled out on the screen as well). Wear headphones and review the videos in a quiet space so as to not disturb others. If you do not have an Internet connection, visit a public library, which should provide free Internet access.
- Purchase an English language learning system, if this is within your budget. These systems can be expensive, and their results depend on the user's commitment as well as the quality of the programme.
- Tips and Warnings

  Be patient, and don't be afraid to make mistakes when speaking.

  Do not buy or register for any English language programmes that promise immediate results, such as speaking English fluently within a month.

Mastering the Art of Conversation

The art of conversation is a skill shared by most successful people. These are people who always seem to rise to the top of their professions and are well respected by others who share the ability to converse with anybody in every situation.

People who seem to speak effortlessly and efficiently with others are generally well liked and highly successful.

If you need to improve your conversational skills, here are a few tips that can help you enhance your conversational skills and boost your image. Good conversation promotes an image of self-confidence, intelligence, and wittiness.

- Always say what you think, not what you think others want you to say. Especially in a professional setting, learning to express your views and ideas in a positive, non-threatening manner will invite reactions and responses.

  Effective leaders always say what they are thinking and express their ideas freely. Having the courage to speak your mind as well as listening openly to the views and ideas of others is a sure way to earn the respect and admiration of all those you encounter.

- Listen carefully to what others are saying. People often interpret things said by others in a way that clouds their ability to hear what people are intending to say.

  By giving your full attention to the speaker, you can hear what they intend for you to hear instead of what you want to hear. The art of conversation includes the ability to listen to others as well as the ability to speak effectively.

- Always assume that a speaker is saying exactly what they mean to say. Even if it seems unclear, try to find meaning and coherence to the words they are saying and give them the respect of hearing what they want you to hear.

  In any conversation, the ability to give respect is just as important as receiving it. The art of conversation is a give and take between parties, not one speaker and one listener.

- Any conversation can be broken down into three parts...

  The first part is small talk. Small talk is dictated by social rules and includes polite greetings, inquiries about the well-being of others, etc.

- Stage two is the end of the small talk and moving on to the purpose of the conversation such as business, the sharing of opinions and personal views.

- Without the ability to express yourself efficiently, the conversation can easily slip back into small talk, lessening the chances of accomplishing the initial goal of the conversation.
- The third part of a conversation is where the various ideas and views expressed can be merged into a satisfying end for all parties involved in the conversation. The art of conversation is a learned skill that is common among successful, energetic people. If you are unable to effectively express yourself in any situation, you will likely find that you do not attract the attention and command the respect that is bestowed upon some others.
- People who talk freely and easily with others usually find more professional and personal fulfilment than those who are introverted and silent.
- If you want to improve your professional and social standing, learn to communicate efficiently and in a positive manner.

  You will notice a dramatic difference in the way other people perceive you if you demonstrate self-confidence and project a friendly, informed image.

General Tips

- Be comfortable with silences
- Try to do most of the talking but do not be overbearing
- Be an active listener
- Stay focussed on the discussion
- Speak slowly and clearly, but naturally, using language appropriate for the topic
- Respect cultural and individual differences

Error Correction Tips

- Ask an expert how and when they want correction
- Celebrate mistakes and praise good work

- Trust your intuition
- Encourage self-correction
- Don't be afraid to say, "I don't know, but I'll find out."
- Focus on only one or two problems at a time
- Focus on meaning and successful communication
- Don't interrupt others in the middle of a thought

Grammar Tips

- Look for problem patterns
- Model the correction: listen to an expert say the entire corrected sentence, and then repeat it
- Check for understanding; talk with an expert about your problem and let him listen to you and correct you
- Keep it simple! Don't get bogged down with technical or lengthy explanations

Vocabulary Tips

- Focus on the new word in context
- Be conscious of using idioms and slang
- Use antonyms and synonyms
- Use facial expressions while talking
- Make sentences using new words you come across

Pronunciation

- Record your voice and hear yourself read
- If possible call and expert to hear you speak and rectify you

How to Have a Great Conversation?

Steps

- Find out about the person you'll be talking to before you actually talk to them, if you can. If it's someone who you work with, or go to school with, look at their department website and see if they have any projects in the works. If the person is a mutual acquaintance, ask your friend what this person does for a living and how they know each other. (Do not, however, dig any deeper than these suggestions. Coming into a conversation equipped with personal information about that person comes off as creepy. That means researching a person on social networks before talking to them for the first time is not okay!) The information you get can be good for starting conversations:

"I was looking at the biochemistry department website and saw that you're working on a pretty interesting thesis! How'd you come to choose that topic?" "I saw on the office memo that you're working on the outreach project for local schools. How's that going?" "Neetu here told me that you went skydiving!"

- Ask questions. What do they like to do? What sort of things have they done in their lives? What is happening to them now? What did they do today or last weekend? Identify things about them that you might be interested in hearing about, and politely ask questions. Remember, there was a reason that you wanted to talk to them, so obviously there was something about them that you found interesting. However, try to space out your questions or they'll feel like you're interrogating them which is very bad and closes off friendships.
- Ask clarifying questions. If the topic seems to be one they are interested in, ask them to clarify what they think or feel about it. If they are talking about an occupation or activity you do not understand, take the opportunity to learn from them. Everyone loves having a chance to teach another willing and interested person about their hobby or subject of expertise. Try to get them talking about something they enjoy thinking about and something that you're interested in hearing or else the conversation isn't fulfilling and one of you will feel unsatisfied with it.
- Listen. This is the most important part of any conversation. Pay attention to what is being said. Make acknowledging noises or movements to indicate that you are still listening. A conversation will go nowhere if you are too busy thinking of

anything else, including what you plan to say next. If you listen well, the other person's statements will suggest questions for you to ask. Allow the other person to do most of the talking. They will often not realise that it was they who did most of the talking, and you get the credit for being a good conversationalist – which of course, you are!

- Practice active listening skills. Part of listening is letting the other person know that you are listening. Make eye contact. Nod. Say "Yes," "I see," "That's interesting," or something similar to give them clues that you are paying attention and not thinking about something else - such as what you are going to say next. Paraphrase back what you have heard, using your own words. This seems like an easy skill to learn, but takes some practice to master. Conversation happens in turns, each person taking a turn to listen and a turn to speak or to respond. It shows respect for the other person when you use your "speaking turn" to show you have been listening and not just to say something new. They then have a chance to correct your understanding, affirm it, or embellish on it.
- Consider your response before disagreeing. If the point was not important, ignore it rather than risk appearing argumentative.

  On the other hand, agreeing with everything can kill a conversation just as easily as disagreeing with everything. When pointing out your difference of opinion, remember these points:
- Agree with something they said (state common ground) before disagreeing.
- Try to omit the word "but" from your conversation when disagreeing, as this word often puts people on the defensive. Instead, try substituting the word "and"—it has less of an antagonistic effect.
- Playing devil's advocate (pretending to defend the opposite point of view) can be a good way to keep the conversation going, but if you overuse this technique, you could end up appearing hostile.

- Don't manipulate the talk to serve your own agenda and steam-roll your counterpart. If you come away from the conversation feeling full of yourself, you used the occasion to show off your wit and knowledge. Try to keep from using a conversation to boost your ego.
- Do not panic over lulls. This is a point where you could easily inject your thoughts into the discussion. If the topic seems to have run out, use the pause to think for a moment and identify another conversation topic or question to ask them. Did something they said remind you of something else you have heard, something that happened to you, or bring up a question or topic in your mind? Mention it and you'll transition smoothly into further conversation!
- Remember that sometimes if a conversation isn't going well, it might not be your fault. Sometimes the other person is distracted/lost in thought, isn't willing to contribute, or is having a bad day. If they don't speak or listen, then they are the ones not using good conversation skills, not you. But in any case, it's still a good idea to strive to do your part as a good conversationalist.
- Know when the conversation is over. Even the best conversations will eventually run out of steam or be ended by an interruption. Smile if you're leaving, tell them it was nice talking to them, and say goodbye. Ending on a positive note will leave a good impression.

Tips

Forget yourself. Rohit once said, "It's much easier to become interested in others than it is to convince them to be interested in you." If you are too busy thinking about yourself, what you look like, or what the other person might be thinking, you will never be able to relax.

The best conversations come from gaining new understanding about the topic discussed or the person. Try to lead into personal stories and anecdotes. These give limitless conversation and are revealing about the character of a person.

It's okay to talk about yourself as long as the person listening is interested and getting new information about you or the topic. People don't like to rehash things they already know or have thought about so try to give a new perspective or way of thinking.

While you want to talk about a topic, make sure you pause in between sentences, which allows for the other person to ask a question to clarify if they understand you and/or for them to interject with a thought of their own. Remember, you want to have a conversation, not be a story-teller. A compliment usually does the trick. For example, "I like your handbag" could lead to a discussion over stores, bags, or anything.

Warnings

Choose carefully when asking personal questions. You do not want to venture into overly personal issues. Even if the other person might be willing to talk about it, you may end up learning things that you really do not want to know. You certainly do not want the other person to think afterward that you coerced them into revealing personal information.

Beware of topics that can be inflammatory – such as religion and politics – and don't venture into them unless you know the person has roughly the same convictions as you, or the circumstances otherwise allow for pleasant discussion. Again, it's fine to disagree and can be nice to talk about differences, but it can also be a quick step toward an argument. Try not to ever cut the person off mid-sentence, or when they naturally pause between sentences (or when trying to remember a detail). It seems disrespectful and it makes it seem like you think that what you have to say is more important than what others have to say. Let the person finish their thoughts and then continue on with thoughts of your own. Don't make a flat statement of opinion without adding, "What do you think about that?" or, "Do you think that could be right?" or, "Is that how you see it?" If you don't give people the chance to make up their own minds, they will contradict you.

How to come up with Good Conversation Topics?

You can instantly become good friends with someone just by having a great conversation with them. Here are some conversation ideas in case you get stuck:

Steps

- Offer a genuine compliment like "I like how you look in those shoes" or "You did a fantastic job with that presentation today" or "I love the way you play the piano". Try to make it a compliment that involves something they did, rather than something they are, because then you can carry the conversation forward by asking them how they did what they did. E.g. "Where did you find the shoes?" or "How did you learn to put together such great presentations?" or "Who taught you to play the piano?" If you tell someone they have beautiful eyes, they can thank you and the conversation ends there.
- Bring up family. Your safest bet here is siblings. Parents can be a touchy subject for people who had troubled upbringings, have estranged parents, or whose parents have recently passed away. The topic of children can be uncomfortable for couples who are having fertility issues or disagreements about whether to have children, or for a person who wants to have kids but hasn't found the right person or situation. So stick with asking about siblings:

  Do you have any siblings?

  How many?

  What are their names?

  How old are they?

  What do your siblings do? (Modify the question based on how old they are.

  Do they go to school/college, have a job? etc.)

  Do you look alike?

  Do you all have similar personalities?

  You could mention a 2008 study which found that the oldest sibling usually has the highest IQ, but younger siblings tend to excel in other areas of life, like sports and arts. If you have siblings, you can say something like "I know that's true/not true for my family when I was growing up, is it true for yours?"

- Ask about their travels. Ask the person where they've been; even if they have never left their home town, you can always ask where they want to go.

  If you had a chance to move to any other country, which one would it be and why?

  Of all the cities in the world you've visited, which one was your favourite?

  Where did you go on your last vacation, and how did you like it?

  What was the best/worst vacation or trip you've ever been on?

- Inquire about food and drink. Food is a little better to talk about because there's always the chance of bumping into someone who has had issues with alcohol abuse, whether they were alcoholics, or they had negative experiences with an alcoholic. So talk about food. Be careful that the conversation doesn't stray into someone going on and on about their diet, how they're trying to lose weight, etc. That can take the conversation in a negative direction.

  Ask "If you could only have one meal for the rest of your life, what would it be?

  "What's your favourite food?

  Where do you like to go when you eat out?

  Do you like to cook?

  What's your favourite kind of candy?

  What's the worst restaurant experience you've ever had?

- Ask about work. This one is especially tricky. Use with care. A date might think you're a gold digger. Or the conversation could end up sounding like a job interview. Still, if you can handle it carefully and keep it short and sweet (and prevent it from turning into a competition over whose job or boss is worse) then here are some starters:

  What was your first job ever?

  Who was your favourite boss in the past and why?

When you were a kid, what did you want to be when you grew up?

What do you like best about your job?

If money was no object, but you still had to work, what would be your dream job?

- Find out about their interests and hobbies. This is where it starts to get more personal. It's up to you to carry the conversation beyond these questions in an appropriate way. Just always remember to stay positive, ask questions, and relate.

  What do you do in your spare time?

  What kind of music do you listen to?

  What kinds of movies do you like to watch?

  What are your favourite TV shows?

  What's your favourite board game or card game?

Tips

Read up on current events. Read the paper and browse social bookmarking sites for current, interesting stories. Be careful with religion and politics though. With some people, this can quickly go awry. Try to stick with something more general.

Listen carefully, and try to relate. After someone has answered, relate your own experience to something they mentioned, or answer the question yourself, even if they don't ask you.

A really good way to keep the conversation going and balanced is to take it in turns to ask questions. It doesn't need to be like a quiz, or a competition to see who can ask the best questions, but it's a gentle way of maintaining a good conversation. Better still, you can introduce some basic rules, such as: The questions can be about anything you like, and if the person doesn't want to answer a question, they don't have to. By saying that, things aren't so awkward if you accidentally ask a sensitive or inappropriate question. If it's your first time talking to the person, try to tie the topic to something related to the situation at hand, rather than just jumping into some random topic.

Warnings

Play it safe and don't talk about any of the following unless you are really good friends with that person:

- Past relationships
- Anything that can be answered with one word
- Politics
- The next date or future dates.
- Religion
- Illness, bad health
- Unpleasant smells
- Job woes (boredom, bad boss, pays, etc.)
- Specialized interests, unless the other person is fascinated and wants to know about it.
- Watch this if you have Asperger syndrome.
- Dark topics like serial killers and stalkers
- Bragging
- Any negative judgements
- Don't just mindlessly work through the list of questions mentioned above. It will certainly make the other person feel interrogated.

How to Have a Witty Conversation?

Being witty is a good way to use your intelligence and knowledge to amuse people. It can also be an impressive flirting tool! But be warned, if the person you're having a conversation with isn't grasping your wittiness, you might come off as a snob, or just plain weird. In that sense, it's a good way to see if you've met your intellectual match.

Steps

- Learn to listen in a different way. One of the tenets of being a good listener is to reflect that what the other person has just said in your own words. It shows that you processed their ideas. In being witty, however, you're going to reflect their words in a different way. You'll be implying that you understand them by comparing their statement to something else. The more "something else" you know, the more comparisons you can make, and the wittier you can be.

- Use creative and vivid exaggeration. Let's say your friend is telling you how cross-eyed his teacher is. You can say, in response, "So she's so cross-eyed that when she cries, the tears run down her back?" Use puns. Take a word or phrase that the other person just used, and use it in a different way that still ties into the conversation. Let's take the example from the previous step: "...the tears run down her back." If you're feeling witty, and there happen to be a pair of stethoscopes around, hold them up mimicking a doctor and say "Evidently a case of bacteria!"

  Of course, if you are a doctor, or even an aspiring one, you don't need to have the prop. If there wasn't any medical context to the conversation, however, the response would be totally random, and not very witty. You can also use a word in a sentence in a way that more than one of its meanings is relevant.

Learn from the masters:

- Read Shakespeare. His use of puns in dialogues is widely regarded.
- Study the characters of the television show "M*A*S*H". An average episode can provide several examples of witty puns, as well as some of the pitfalls in overusing them.
- Use metaphors. Let's say someone says, out of the blue, "It's 6 o'clock!" You can say "Thank you, Big Ben!" ("Big Ben" is a nickname for a giant bell in a clock in London.) This is a particularly sarcastic example, because you're also implying (by saying "thank you") that you didn't care to know what time it was (because you're obviously not thankful!) but not all metaphors have to be sarcastic. Describing a messy desk, for instance, as the "North Pacific Gyre" is a witty and creative

way to say it's quite messy. You can also use witty metaphors to compliment or admire someone.

- Respond with a relevant quotation from a movie, book, or significant figure. The more obscure the reference, the wittier the statement—but the greater the confusion if the person you're talking to doesn't know what you're referring to. If someone says "I'll try" and you say "Do or do not; there is no try." —they may, or may not, realise that you're making a Star Wars reference.
- Reply quickly and nonchalantly. The wittiness is not only in how creatively you can link ideas and draw comparisons, but also in how quickly. And keeping your witty remarks in a casual tone makes it look like it was so easy. A playful smile and a raised eyebrow can also add a nice touch!
- Think about everything before it happens! If you already have a response to something before it happens then when (and if) it happens it will seem like it was easier for you to think of a response. Just make sure that you pay attention to what actually happened and if your response makes sense BEFORE you say/do it.

Warnings

- Using your wittiness to put people down without them realising is low. (This is the pun referred to earlier. It's moralistically "low" and also figuratively "low" because you put someone down.)
- Use your comments sparingly. If suddenly everyone hears the same references over and over again, they will start to doubt your wittiness and intelligence.
- Some aggressively witty individuals may take your use of wit in a conversation as an invitation to engage in a "battle of wits". While this can be an enjoyable and engaging activity, it also has the potential to seem personal. Be prepared to set your limits and respect the limits of others to avoid hurt feelings.
- There is such a thing as being too witty – there is indeed a fine

balance between making witty conversation and just showing off and alienating the person (or people) you're talking to.

How to Start a Conversation when you have nothing to talk about?

Whether you're a host or a guest, there are loads of social situations that will call for interaction, even when you're stumped for some way to oil the wheels of conversation. The seeming inability to start a conversation when you've nothing to talk about is partly about nerves, partly about talking yourself into believing that you have nothing in common with the other person, and partly an unwillingness to try the new or even to put in the effort.

Overcome the nerves and the lukewarm desire to find ways of conversing with others you might never have tried before, and become a lot more comfortable around people in a conversational setting. Here are some suggestions to help.

Steps

- Begin by introducing yourself. It's very simple, and consists of telling the new person your name, offering your hand to shake and smiling.
- Be aware of your internal monologue. When you suddenly feel that you're not able to engage in conversation with another person, it's likely that you're telling yourself a few negative things, such as worrying that you're boring, not good enough, too unimportant, intruding, wasting their time, etc. You might also be worrying about what the other person is thinking about you and this concern causes you to feel tongue-tied. Feeling self-conscious when carrying on conversation with others is not unusual but it's also not productive. Try to keep in mind that everyone has these self-doubts from time to time but that it's essential to overcome them in order to engage with fellow human beings.
- Reassure yourself that the other person is not judging you. Even if they are, think "So what?" and don't give them the upper hand in your life. Realise that there are many good

ways to leap over your negative inner monologue and to fire up the conversation. It's an art which can be learned, and requires practice.

- Understand the secret to a good conversation. The secret at the heart of a good conversation is to listen and do very little of the talking, apart from encouraging the other person to open up. Once you understand this, you should feel a lot more reassured. Of course, there is an art to getting this happening but it's not hard. The process follows these two steps:

  Make a general comment about the location or occasion. Look around and see if there is anything worth pointing out. Examples of location or occasion comments: "What an amazing room!" or "Such incredible catering!" or "I love this view!" or "Great dog!"Ask an open question and get them talking about themselves.

- Know how to ask an open question. Most people love to talk about themselves; it's your place as the conversation starter to get them going. An open question is a question that requires an explanation for an answer, and not just a simple "Yes" or "No" as is commonly answered to a closed question. Open questions tend to begin with: Who? When? What? Why? Where? and How? Closed questions (are you? do you? have you?) only bring you back to the point of not knowing how to get the conversation going, whereas open questions oil the conversation and have the other person doing the talking.

  A closed question: "Do you like books?", "Have you been to university?", "Is spring your favourite season?", "Am I intruding?" "Do you come here often?"An open question: "What sort of books do you like?", "What did you study at university?", "Which is your favourite season? Why?", "What are you doing right now?", "Where's your usual watering hole?"

- That's a great hairdo you've got there! Where d'ya get it done? Put the location comment together with the open question and your conversation will be underway. For example:

"That's a nice handbag, where did you get it?". This lets the handbag owner talk about the day that they went shopping and all this funny stuff happened, as opposed to, "I like your handbag." "Thank you." and then it's over."What an amazing buffet! Which is your favourite dish?" This lets the other person open up about food likes and anticipation of eating. "Fantastic turn out! Which of the lecturers is your favourite?"

"I love your costume. Which are your favourite Horror movies?"

When you first meet people, it's important to keep the conversation light and simple. Rely on small talk until the two of you get to know one another better, as this is a time when you're both trying to establish rapport and similarities rather than setting each other up for an opinionated argument.

Small talk encompasses such topics as your blog or website, the purchase of a new car, house renovations, your kids' artwork prize, vacation plans, your newly planted garden, a good book you've just read, etc. Small talk is not politics, religion, nuclear disarmament or fusion, or criticizing anybody, especially not the host or the event you're both attending. And although talking about the weather is a cliché, if there's something unusual about the weather, you've got a great topic of conversation. And how did that make you feel? Use words of a sensory nature. These are words such as "see", "imagine", "feel", "tell", "sense", etc., in order to encourage the other person to keep painting a descriptive picture as part of their conversation.

For example: Where do you see yourself in a year's time? What's your sense of the current stock market fluctuations? How do you feel about the new plans for renovating downtown? What do you imagine he was thinking when he asked for a pay rise higher than the boss's salary?

Remember to synchronise. Once your partner-in-conversation has started talking, follow his or her cue to keep the conversation going smoothly. Use active listening to reflect what they're saying and to summarize their possible feelings.

Say the other person's name now and then. Not only does it help you to remember them but it's a warming sign of respect and mutual like. Give encouraging feedback. You don't even have to say things a lot of the time - nod, say ah-ha or wow or oh or hmm, sigh, grunt convivially, and short encouraging statements such as "Is that so?" and "Goodness!", and "What did you do/say then?" and "That's amazing!", etc. Keep your body language open and receptive. Nod in agreement, make occasional genuine eye contact without staring, and lean in toward the other person. Place your hand on your heart now and then, and even touch them on the upper arm if you're a touchy, feely person.

Keep good thoughts going through your head. Stay interested in the other person and focused on them. Keep your curiosity piqued rather than walking down the path of dark self-consciousness and withdrawing back into yourself. Note each time a similarity or common goal pops up in the conversation to remind yourself of the worth of continuing to connect with this person. Smile a lot, and laugh when any quip is made by the other person.

Notice signs of not wanting to talk, such as grimacing, screwing up face, etc. Respond thoughtfully to someone who remains awkward or uncomfortable in your presence. If your conversation partner appears withdrawn and uninterested in sharing information with you, don't persist too much. Try a little more before making a decision to move on.

Keep your questions non-invasive; be sure you're not asking them questions they'd rather not discuss. For example, some people might be very uncomfortable discussing issues that they feel touch on them personally, such as weight, lack of having a degree or qualifications, lack of having a steady date, etc. Try to be as thoughtful as possible even though you don't really know them yet. Don't ask too many questions if your conversation partner continues to appear unresponsive.

Maintain the equilibrium. As the person who started the conversation, the responsibility initially rests with you to maintain the momentum. But what about when the other person starts practicing active listening and open questions back on you? You have several options:

Relish it as their cue to let you start talking about yourself. Just don't overdo it and remember to keep engaging them back with open questions and active listening at the end of your own recounting.

Deflect it if you'd rather not be the center of conversation attention. Say something like: "Well, I like Harry Potter books, and I especially loved the last one. But you don't want to hear about me all night! What were your favourite moments in the Harry Potter series?"Answer questions with a question. For example, "How did you manage to get away so early?" could be responded to with a: "Well, how did you?". Often the other person will be so intent on filling you in on their side of the story that they'll forget they asked you the question first!

Practice getting conversations started. You may feel a little clumsy at first, but with practice it can become easy to start good conversations. Every time you're in a situation where you're called upon to converse with others, see it as part of your ongoing practice, and note how you're improving each time that you try it.

Tips

Speak with clarity and purpose. If you're mumbling, it makes conversing a lot harder.

Show interest in the conversation.

Reflect before speaking if it's your turn to talk and allow silence to also have its rightful place in your conversation. Don't be afraid of pauses – use them to change topics, re-energize the conversation, or to take a short breather even.

Relax. Chances are that whatever small-talk you're making isn't going to stick out in anyone's mind a few months from now. Just say whatever comes into your head, so long as it's not offensive or really weird (unless, of course, the person you're attempting to converse with is into weird stuff). If you think of something in your head while you're talking, it's probably related.

It will help if you watch some TV, listen to radio shows, and/or read a lot – newspapers, magazines, and/or books. Doing this will ensure that you have some idea of what's going on in the world.

Remember and plan to share anything you like, think is funny, or find intriguing. This is a way of building up your own inner library of things that might be helpful to another person during a conversation someday. It can be amazing how you thread these interesting things when you least expect it, and make conversation an adventure instead of a dreadful task. If you take it to the next step and say things that you want the person to think of as adding value, and keep to yourself things that the person might not, you're actually honing your own personality to be appealing to the other person, and what is a greater act of kindness than that?

If you're shy, it is helpful to have thought about a topic or two in advance that you feel comfortable talking about.

A great entry into starting a conversation, especially for a guy approaching a girl, is to mention you can only talk briefly as you're meeting up with other friends. This relieves the girl of any fear of being uncomfortably stuck with someone she does not know, and gives you both an easy out if things don't progress well. If the conversation does progress well, you can always delay leaving your new friend for as long as you like. Remember not to overdo it, because she might think that you don't want to talk to her, but prefer to be with your friends.

Follow the lead that your listener is expressing. If he or she appears interested, then continue. If he or she is looking at a clock or watch, or worse, looking for an escape strategy, then you've been going on for too long.

Interesting and funny quotes or facts can lighten things up, and make way for things to talk about. You could also use a set of conversation starter question cards for inspiration.

If talking over the phone, keep the person involved in the conversation at all costs. If you can't come up with a good topic, try the "questions" game. Just keep asking them questions; random questions work just fine as long as they are appropriate. This technique can save a phone conversation. The questions should be open ended questions that do not require a yes or no answer. For example "How do you know the hosts?" This way you can ask questions about what they just said or follow up with how you know the hosts (for example) instead of acting as if the conversation is an interrogation.

Half of an effective conversation is the way you non-verbally communicate, and not necessarily what you say. Practice better non-verbal skills that are friendly and confident.

Take a mental note of some amusing things that you saw or heard throughout the day. For example, something funny someone said, a fun activity you did with your friends, or anything interesting. This can give way to future conversation.

Watch some stand-up comedians or comedy shows to get an idea of how to start a conversation humourously. Usually, the leads you find will be funny, and you will not need much in common to talk about them.

Remember, whoever you are talking to, you always have something in common. We all experience the weather, like good food, and enjoy a good laugh. When in doubt, just talk to them about what they are there for. For example, if you meet them at a bus stop, ask them where they are going. If they are from out of town, ask them about their life at home.

To break the ice, a compliment is always nice.

People like to hear "hey, you look like my cousin!" or "Are you by any chance related to...?" They could be great conversation starters.

Warnings

- Don't be overly invasive with your questions.
- Watch out if you use tons of fillers like "umm" or "soo". It might make the person you're talking to feel awkward or obligated to say something. Instead talk slowly and pause. This will create a little tension and make your newly found friend more invested in your conversation.
- Don't ever comment negatively on the person with whom you are talking, or anyone else; you never know if there is a personal attachment to the person you are criticizing.

Never swear, insult, disrespect, use racial, religious, sexual orientation, and gender slurs in front of others (unless you know who they are and if they have the same views on things as you).

- Never act arrogantly and pretend to be a Know-It-All when dealing with people.
- Never ever interrupt a conversation between one or more people. Wait for the conversation to stop and then say something. Common courtesy goes a long way.
- Make use of "please", "may I", "thank you", "could you" when someone is nice to you and when you want something. Being polite shows maturity and intelligence.
- Don't always talk about your financial status in the presence of your new friend, especially when a guy has met with a girl.
- Also remember that not everyone wants to talk. If the person shows signs of discomfort or loss of interest, you should not bother them

How to Join a Conversation?

Joining people in the middle of conversation can be a tricky task. You could even be termed as rude or impudent if the timing and what you say is not appropriate.

Steps

- Listen to what they are saying, and when it's appropriate, give your opinion on whatever they're talking about or ask a question. If you don't know what they are talking about but it sounds interesting, ask them about it. Asking people what they're talking about can sometimes just annoy them and make them want to avoid you because you aren't a part of their social group. Understand these boundaries and don't try to butt into any conversation you hear.
- Continue in the conversation as if you were already part of it, and hopefully they won't have a problem with you joining. It is often best to start with a small comment and judge the reaction before continuing. Be Careful. If they're talking about

a subject that you are familiar with, then gently put in your input. DO NOT cut someone off to say what you need to say. If you don't understand ask one of your friends in the group to explain it to you.

Tips

- If you walk in on a conversation and have no clue what they're talking about, don't say anything until you've figured out what they're talking about.
- If you know the people who are talking they will be more likely to let you join. However, if anyone hints to go away, you should.
- Try to see what kind of conversation it is before jumping in. Personal conversations are best avoided, and do not linger near one too long, as you might be deemed nosy.
- Try to read the body language of the people talking. Before you join, see if the people are talking closely or in hushed tones; if it seems to be a serious conversation, you might want to leave them alone.
- If the group seems more open, take the opening. If the members of the conversation try to nudge you out, take the hint and assume the conversation was personal in nature.

Warnings

- The biggest conversation-killer is self-consciousness. Don't worry about saying something stupid; it happens to all of us at some point. The worst thing you can do is to not speak up when there is a fitting opportunity.
- Do not repetitively barge in on a conversation, or else you might be considered nosy, and that will likely be used against you when you try to join future conversations.
- Do not barge in on a personal conversation, as you probably will receive negative feedback from the conversers.
- Sometimes, even if you do join the conversation appropriately, some or all of the people involved will still be irritated and try to push you out. If so, that is their problem, and you should

probably not bother trying to join their conversations again; it isn't worth it.

How to make the Conversation Flow?

Who says that making small talk with new people has to be awkward? Here's some advice for getting a conversation started and keeping awkward silence at bay.

Steps

- Introduce yourself with a smile. Then ask a person for his or her name. Reply with: "It is nice to meet you, [fill in his/her name]."
- Ask questions that will help you find common ground. For example, what's his or her favourite sport? Share what you like about that sport, too. This strategy works well with both kids and grown-ups.
- Be positive. If your new acquaintance, says "bowling" and you loathe bowling, keep it to yourself. Ask what she likes about bowling. You may be intrigued by the answer!
- Ask open-ended questions. Asking how she first became interested in bowling, for example, will carry your conversation longer than, "How long have you been playing?"
- Stay focused on the other person. She will appreciate what a good listener you are!

Tips

Still at a loss for what to say? Try one of these guaranteed conversation starters:

"If you could invite any five famous people to dinner, living or dead, who would you choose and why?"

"You can only eat one food for the rest of your life, what would it be?"

"What kind of animal do you identify with most? Why?"

"What would you do with the money if you won the lottery?"

"What do you think the most interesting fortune cookie might say?"

Make good eye contact. Look at the person who is talking—not as his buttons or the way his ears stick out.

Nod your head now and then to show that you are listening and interested, and to give encouragement to the talker to continue.

Conversations are about taking turns talking. Give the other person his turn, and when it's your turn, speak up.

How to Start an Interesting Conversation?

Ever tried to have a conversation with someone who completely bores you? Or noticed how your story about Lassie has got the person half asleep? Here are some tips to make a conversation more interesting.

Steps

- Think of the other person. Hopefully you would know the person enough to know things about them. Do they skateboard? Are they getting their masters degree? Try asking them questions like "What tricks can you do?" or "And what are you planning to do after you get your degree?"
- Smile. It makes you naturally happier. When you're happy, you're not going to fall asleep when someone goes on endlessly about their golf game.
- When you tell a story, or share something - use humour (but don't laugh throughout the whole thing let them laugh first). Your goal is to make people interested, not to fill them with facts. Sliding in a joke or making a brief sarcastic compliment makes you seem more approachable, and the people will be more comfortable speaking to you. When you're comfortable, you wouldn't mind listening to Grandpa's old war stories.
- Keep your story short. Try to keep it from 30 seconds to 2 minutes. Anything longer has the person uninterested.
- Ask questions. If you didn't understand something, or the person's story was lame, ask a question that would lead to an interesting story – "Have you ever gotten hurt when you were

riding on your skateboard?" And then you might hear some pretty cool things. Of course, only ask questions about things that would interest you.

- If they are boring you to death, and there are no more resorts, then make an excuse and leave. Say that you have to go, that your cell phone just went off, anything. Be polite, say "It was nice talking to you," and get out of there.

Tips

- Ask questions. People love telling stories. Ask them about their experiences, whether it be about a movie or about how they got hurt.
- Keep your responses short. Don't give detail after detail about how you studied for 5 hours.
- Say that you studied for 5 hours, don't give a play by play.
- Be polite. Try to stay away from Politics or Religion.
- Enjoy yourself.
- Smile
- If they're boring, make them interesting. Change the subject. If you're bored out of your mind, ask them about something that you like – music, friends, movies, etc.
- Be polite.
- If you change the subject too much or too suddenly, it will be regarded as rude. If someone is really boring you, try changing the subject slightly. If the subject is golf, for example, try changing it to the Olympics.

Warnings

- Don't be boring!
- Believe in yourself!
- Don't make them think you're boring!
- Be polite the whole time. (Even in humourous matters)
- Don't even make a joke and then actually insult them!

CHAPTER 2

Ways to Improve English Conversation

Whether you are conversant in written English or not, you still need to develop certain skills to be able to converse fluently in the language.

Here are a few tips to help you improve English conversational skills.

- Start your own English language blog.

  Even for people who don't have to write in English, writing can be a great way of properly learning the kind of vocabulary you need to describe your own life and interests, and of thinking about how to stop making grammar mistakes. The problem most people have is that they don't know what to write about. One traditional way to make sure you write every day in English is to write an English diary (journal), and a more up to date way of doing this is to write a blog. Popular topics include your language learning experience, your experience studying abroad, your local area, your language, or translations of your local news into English.

- Write a news diary.

  Another daily writing task that can work for people who

would be bored by writing about their own routines in a diary is to write about the news that you read and listen to everyday. If you include your predictions for how you think the story will develop, this can give you a good reason to read old entries another time, at which time you can also correct and mistakes you have made and generally improve what you have written.

- Sign up for a regular English tip.

  Some websites offer a weekly or even daily short English lesson sent to your email account. If your mobile phone has an e-mail address, it is also possible to have the tips sent to your phone to read on the way to work or school. Please note, however, that such services are not usually graded very well to the levels of different students, and they should be used as a little added extra or revision in your English studies rather than as a replacement for something you or your teacher have chosen more carefully as what you need to learn.

- Listen to MP3s.

  Although buying music on the internet is becoming more popular in many countries, not so many people know that you can download speech radio such as audio books (an actor reading out a novel) and speech radio. Not only is this better practice for your English than listening to English music, from sources like Channel 'V', HBO, BBC and Australia's ABC Radio.

- Listen to English music.

  Even listening to music while doing something else can help a little for things like getting used to the natural rhythm and tone of English speech, although the more time and attention you give to a song the more you will learn from listening to it again in the future.

- Read the lyrics to a song.

  Although just listening to a song in English can be a good way of really learning the words of the chorus in an easily memorable way, if you want to really get something out of listening to English music you will need to take some time to read the lyrics of the song with a dictionary. If the lyrics are not given in the CD booklet, you may be able to find them on the internet, but please note that some lyrics sites deliberately put a few errors into their lyrics for copyright reasons. Once you have read and understood the lyrics, if you then listen and read at the same time, this can be a good way of understanding how sounds change in fast, natural, informal speech.

- Sing karaoke in English.

  The next stage after understanding and memorising a song is obviously to sing it. Although some words have their pronunciation changed completely to fit in with a song, most of the words have the same sounds and stressed syllables as in normal speech. Remembering which words rhyme at the end of each line can also be a good way of starting to learn English pronunciation.

- Write a film, music, hotel or book review.

  Another motivating and easy way to make yourself write in English is to write a review for a site such as Amazon or Internet Movie Database. Many non-native speakers write reviews on sites like this, and if you have some special understanding of the book, music or film due to your first language or knowing the artist personally, that would be very interesting for the English speakers who read and write reviews on the site.

- Only search in English.

  Switching your search engine to the English language version of msn, yahoo, Google etc. cannot only be a good way of practising fast reading for specific information in English, but could also give you a wider choice of sites to choose from and give you an idea of what foreigners are writing about your country and area.

- Read a book you've already read or seen the movie of in your own language.

  Although most language learners under Advanced level would

probably learn more from reading a graded reader or something from the internet than they would from reading an original book written for English speakers, for some people reading something like Harry Potter in the original can be a great motivator to improve their English. To make this easier for you and make sure that it motivates you rather than just making your tired, try reading a book that you already know the story of. This not only makes it easier to understand and guess vocabulary, but you are also more likely to remember the language in it. If you have not read the book before, reading a plot summary from the internet can also help in the same way.

- Read a translation into English.

  Another way of making sure books are easier to understand is to choose a book that was originally translated into English, preferably from your own language. Even if you haven't read the book in your own language, you will find the English is written in a slightly simplified way that is more similar to how your own language is written than a book originally written in English would be.

- Skip the first ten pages.

  If you have given up with a book in English or are reading it very slowly, try skimming through the first ten pages or skipping them completely. The start of most books tend to be mainly description and are therefore full of difficult vocabulary and don't have a clear story line yet to help you understand what is happening and to motivate you to turn the next page. If the book is still too difficult even after the introductory part is finished, it is probably time to give that book up for now and try it again after you have read some easier things.

- Read a book with lots of dialogue.

  Opening up books before you buy one and flicking through them to find one with lots of direct dialogue in it has several advantages. If there is less text on the page due to all the speech marks etc, this can make it easier to read and easier to write translations on. Dialogue is also much easier to understand than descriptive parts of a book, and is much more like the language you will want to learn in order to be able to speak English.

- Read English language comics.

  Even more than books with lots of dialogue, comics can be easy to understand and full of idiomatic language as it is actually spoken. There can be difficulties with slang, difficult to understand jokes and/ or dialogue written how people speak rather than with normal spellings, so try to choose which comic carefully. Usually, serious or adventure comics are easier to understand than funny ones.

- Read English language entertainment guides.

  Nowadays most big cities in the world have an English language magazine and/ or online guide to the movies, plays, exhibitions that are on in the city that week. Reading this in English is not only good value, but it could also guide you to places that English speakers are interested in and where you might hear some English spoken around you.

- Read English language magazines.

  Like books, if you can read two versions of the same magazine (Newsweek in your language and in English, for example), that could make understanding it much easier.

- Take a one week intensive course.

  Although you cannot expect to come out of a very short course speaking much better English than when you started it, if you continue studying a little over the following weeks and months, the knowledge you gained then will gradually come out and mean that your level of speaking, listening etc. are better than they would have been if you hadn't taken that course. This positive effect can still be true up to a year later.

- Follow your intensive course up with an extensive course.

  The more time you can spend studying English the better, but studying periodic intensive courses with a few hours of study a week in between is probably better value for money than any other system as it gives your brain time to subconsciously learn and start using the new language you have learnt before you introduce the next new "chunk" of language.

- Supplement your group class with a one to one class.

  Another good way to combine two different kinds of classes is to study both in a group class and one to one. Having a one to one teacher, even if just a couple of times a month, will mean that you can be taught exactly the language that you need, that you will have more time to speak, and that you can have as much error correction as you like.

- Supplement your one to one class with a group class.

  The benefits of having a group class are often less clear to students, but they include the fact that you will learn to deal with several people speaking at once, have a chance to practice skills such as interrupting people, and will hear a range of different viewpoints and topics.

- Teach your children or friends some English.

  Recent research has shown that elder children tend to be a couple of IQ points above their younger siblings, and the most likely reason is that explaining things to their little brothers and sisters gives them an intellectual boost. In the same way, teaching someone lower level than you the English you already know is a great way of permanently fixing that knowledge in your own brain.

- Ask your company to start English lessons.

  Even if you don't need to speak English at work, English lessons can be a fun and reasonably priced way for your company to spend their training budget in a popular way.

- Have English radio on in the background while you are doing your housework. Even if you are not listening carefully, it will help you get a feel for natural English rhythm and intonation.

- Play English language learning games on your computer.

  Although such games can have quite random language and

are unlikely to improve your ability to speak English on their own, the next time you hear or read the same language elsewhere it will be really fixed in your brain by the fact you have played a game with it in already. It is also a nice way of taking a break from your other English studies while also doing some English. To make sure it really is a break and to avoid wasting time learning language from the game that is not much used in daily life, don't bother writing down any new language you see in the game, but just try to learn it from playing the game again.

- Say or think what you are doing in English as you do your daily tasks.

  As you are doing your chores, try creating sentences describing what you are doing, e.g. 'I am unscrewing the ketchup bottle cap'. This gets you used to thinking in English without translating, and can be a good way of seeing what simple vocabulary that is around you everyday you don't know. yet

- Watch English language films with English subtitles.

  For people who can't understand a film without subtitles but find themselves not listening at all when reading subtitles in their own language, this should be the way of watching a film that you should aim for. If it is too difficult to watch the whole film this way, try watching the (usually important) first 10 or 15 minutes of the film with subtitles in your own language, switch to English subtitles after that, and only switch back to subtitles in your own language if you get totally lost following the story of the film.

- Watch films in your language with English subtitles.

  If you are finding English films with English subtitles too difficult or you can't find English films with English subtitles in your local video shop, this is a good second best option. Looking for local films with English subtitles can also sometimes be a good sign of quality, as it means the producers of the film are expecting it to be popular internationally as well.

- Watch English films with subtitles in your language.

  Again, this is not as good practice as English language films with English subtitles, but is more relaxing, can be easier to find suitable DVDs for, and is also possible with VHS.

- Watch the same film or TV episode over and over again.

  This can not only save you money on DVDs, but will mean that you can really learn the language without having to study it. Some comedies can also get funnier the more you watch them, especially if you watch them with no subtitles and so understand a little more each time you watch it.

- Be realistic about your reading level.

  Most researchers agree that people learn most when reading something they understand almost all of. If there are one or two words per page that you have never seen before, that is about the right level. If there are three or more on every page, you should switch to something easier and come back later.

- Read graded readers (= easy readers).

  These are books that are especially written for language learners like you, e.g. Penguin Readers. Although it can be difficult to find something as interesting as things written in newspapers or on the internet, in terms of learning the language only people who need to read for their work or an exam usually gain more from reading things written for graded readers. Graded readers of classic books like Charles Dickens also have the benefit of giving you a lot of knowledge about the literature, and culture more generally, of English speaking countries in a short time.

- Read the whole thing with no help.

  Although using a dictionary has been shown to help with both short term and long term learning of vocabulary, the fact that using it slows reading down can stop some people reading in English at all. Reading a whole book quickly through just for pleasure from time to time will help you remember how fun reading in another language can be.

- Read and learn everything.

  At the opposite extreme, it can be hard work but very satisfying to get to the end of a book knowing that you have learnt every word in it.

- Watching English children's films or TV programmes.

  Although some of the vocabulary you can learn from things made for children can be a bit strange (lots of animal names and maybe animal noises, including baby names for things), the fact that not only the language but the structure of the story is simplified can make it an easy and motivating thing to watch. Like good language learning materials, the same language is also often repeated to make it memorable, and the use of catchy songs etc. can increase this positive effect on your memory.

- Read English children's books.

  This is very similar to watching English children's movies, but with the added advantage of there being more illustrations than adult books, which both helps you to understand the story and makes the page brighter and more motivating to read.

- Keep a list of language to learn, e.g. a vocab list.

  Even if you don't often find time to go through your vocab list and it keeps on building up, just the act of choosing which words you need to learn and writing them down on a special list can help you learn them.

- Go through your vocab list several times every day.

  If ticking off words on a vocabulary list on the train to work is inconvenient or embarrassing for you, you can keep your list of words to learn as an entry in your electronic dictionary, as a mobile phone to do list or as a text file in your MP3 player (e.g. iPod). Although the time spent transferring the information between different formats like these may seem wasted, in fact any time you spend using the vocabulary like this will help you learn it.

- Convert your vocab list to English only.

  One way to stop yourself translating and therefore increase your speed of comprehension and production is to learn all your vocabulary without the use of your own first language. Ways you can write a vocab list in only English include with synonyms (words with the same meaning, e.g. "tall" and "high"); with opposites ("high" and "low"); with pronunciation factors such as number of syllables (the number of beats, e.g. three for "de- ci- sion") and the word stress (the syllable that is pronounced louder and longer, e.g. the second syllable in "baNAna"); and gapped sentences (e.g. "I am not ________________ in science fiction" for the word "interested").

- Cross out and delete.

  Crossing out or deleting words, sentences or whole pages that you have learnt can be a great motivator, and save your list of things to learn becoming too big to handle.

- Throw everything away and start again.

  One of the things that can put most people off learning is a stack of half finished books or a huge list vocabulary waiting to be learnt. Simply getting rid of all that and starting again with something new from zero can be a great motivator and get your studies underway again.

- Label things in your house or office with post-its.

  The easiest vocabulary to learn is the vocabulary of things you see and use every day. If you can write the names of things around you on slips of paper and stick them on the real thing, this is a great way of learning useful vocabulary. If you can leave them there over the following days and weeks, this is a very easy way of revising the vocabulary until it is properly learnt.

- Label a drawing.

  For people who can't put labels on real things, the next best option is to take a photo of a real place in your life like your office, print it out, and then draw lines to all of the things you can see in the picture and label them in English with the help of a dictionary. You can do the same thing with places you pass through everyday like the station. Because you will see the same thing again and again, it should be easy to really learn the words for those things.

- Keep a diary in English.

  This is a popular method of making sure you use English everyday for people who don't often speak English and can't think of things to write about. The fact that you are writing about real things that have happened to you means that any words you look up in the dictionary will be vocabulary that is useful for you and easy to learn.

- Online chat.

  The closest thing to speaking for people who don't have the chance to speak English is online chat, as you have to think and respond quickly, and the language is short and informal just like speech.

- **Listen to the radio news in English.** You can make this easier by reading the news in English first, or even just by reading or listening to the news in your own language.

- Read an English language newspaper.

  Read Freebie newspapers they are usually the easiest to understand, followed by The Times of India, The Hindustan Times.

- Write fiction in English, e.g. short stories.

  For people who find writing a diary about things that happen to them everyday boring, the best thing is to let your imagination go and write about whatever comes into your head. The advantage of this is that if you can't think of how to say something in English, you can just change the story to something that is easier to explain. Perhaps the easiest way to start writing fiction in English is with a diary, changing any details you like to make it more interesting and adding more and more fantasy as the weeks go on.

- English language exercise videos.

  This is quite similar to how babies learn, by listening, watching and copying. It is also good for your health!

- Learn a famous speech or poem in English by heart.

  Although you may never hear or get the chance to say exactly that line, having one memorable example of an English grammatical form in your head can make it much easier to learn other examples of the same grammar as you hear them. It is also something you can practice over and over without being as boring as grammatical drills.

- Use a dictionary while you are watching a movie.

  Films often have the same words many times, so if you look up important words the first or second time you hear them, you should have learnt them by the end of the film. It is easier to use a dictionary if you watch with English subtitles.

- Learn and use the phonemic script.

  Although there are many sounds in English, there are even more spellings. By learning the phonemic script and writing vocabulary down with it, you can both add another stage to your vocabulary learning that should help you learn it more thoroughly, and improve your pronunciation. It can also make things easier for you by stopping you trying to pronounce different spellings of the same pronunciation different ways.

- Learn some spelling rules.

  Many people think that English spelling is random, but in fact most words follow some kind of rule, e.g. the "magic E" that changes the pronunciation of "mad" and "made".

- Record your own voice. For people who don't have much or any correction of pronunciation from a teacher, recording yourself and listening back makes it easier to hear whether you are really making the English sounds that you are trying to or not.

- Use computer pronunciation analysis.

  Although most programmes that claim to tell you when you

are pronouncing correctly or not don't actually do that, listening many times and seeing how your voice changes as you try to match the sounds and waveform given by a pronunciation CD ROM can be good practice and more motivating than just recording your own voice.

- Learn as many words as you can of one category, e.g. animal words.

  Learning similar words together can both expand your overall vocabulary and make them easier to learn by forming links between the words in your brain.

- Take holidays abroad.

  This is not only a good opportunity to speak English in situations where you really have to make yourself understood in order to live, but it is also a good motivator to study English seriously in the weeks and months before your trip. If possible, also try to use English even when you could use your own language, e.g. when you pick a guided tour of a museum or historic place or when you book a flight on the internet, and try to avoid package tours.

- Draw pictures of the words you want to learn.

  Especially if you are artistic, this can be a better way of learning vocabulary than writing translations or example sentences.

- Find a foreign boyfriend or girlfriend.

  No tips on how to do this here, but everyone agrees that getting or even just looking for a date in English can be a great motivator to improve your language skills.

- Arrange a conversation exchange.

  Swapping lessons and conversation with someone who wants to learn your language can be a good alternative for those who aren't looking for romance, or can sometimes lead onto dating for those who are!

- Model your accent on one particular actor. e.g. try to speak like Robert De Niro.

  Students who say they want to sound more like a native

speaker have the problem that native speakers don't sound all that much like each other. Choosing one model can make the task of improving your pronunciation more clear, and is quite fun. Doing an impression of that person also makes a good party trick.

- Use an English-English dictionary.

  Trying to use a bilingual dictionary less and switching to a monolingual one can help you to stop translating in you head when you are speaking or listening, and other useful English vocabulary can come up while you are using the dictionary.

- Occasionally talk to or e-mail your friends in English.

  Many people find this a bit false or embarrassing, but if you think of it as a study club and set a particular time and/ or place, it is no different from studying maths together.

- Go to an English or Irish pub.

  As well as having a menu in English and being a good way of finding out something about the culture of English speaking countries, you might also find there are free English language listings magazines, English language sports on the TV and/ or foreign people you can speak to.

- Buy a speaking electronic dictionary.

  Although most electronic dictionaries are not as good as paper ones for the amount of information they give you about each word, some of them have the very useful function of saying the word with the correct pronunciation.

- Learn your electronic dictionary vocabulary list.

  Most electronic dictionaries also have a button which you can push to see the last 30 or more words you looked up. By deleting words you decide are useless or you have already learnt from this list, you can use it as a "to do list" of words to learn that you can look at several times a day in the train etc.

- Switch operating system to English.

  Changing the operating language of your mobile phone, video

recorder etc. to English can be an easy way of making sure you use the language everyday.

- Set goals.

  Deciding how many hours you want to study, how many words you want to learn or what score you want to get in a test are all good ways of making sure you do extra study.

- Buy an electronic dictionary, which speaks.

  Understanding of the terms is not adequate. Although you need to know, how the words are pronounced. Speaking dictionary will not just find a word for you; it will also speak it for you. Today no one is bothered to suspect words from the ordinary dictionaries, as it takes time to find words alphabetically. But in electronic dictionaries you type and it shows. You press speak it speaks. As simple as that.

- Start you own Blog.

  Blogging has considered being a great way to improve English online. Blog is a place, where you write anything on any topic you like. For example, write stories, articles, reviews of books, movies, music, etc, write about yourself, like what do you do every day and what unusual and surprising occurs. Join communities and add other blog members into your blog. It enables them and you to see what they are posting and what you are posting in your blogs. Read their posts and comment if you like them.

- Newspapers –

  Reading newspaper is one of the greatest ways ever considered. While you are improving your English reading newspapers, at the same time you know what's been happening in the world. Underline the words you don't understand and keep reading. Its time to find the meaning of the words you'd underlined. Write their meanings against them in a bracket and read it again.

- Read news online –

  If you have a computer at home, then you don't need to waste your money buying newspapers. Every Newspaper has established his websites over the internet. Search for the latest news, print that news, read it, underline difficult words, find their meanings from the dictionary, write them against each underlined term, and read it.

- Signup for a regular English tip website –

  There are many websites over the internet that e-mail you free English tips every day. Signup for them and lift the advantage of them.

  Listen to English mp3 music along their lyrics – If you have an iPod or any mp3 player, then it's great. Remove all the songs that are in your language and upload some English songs instead. Print their lyrics and sing along the song.

- Environment – This is very important that you change the environment a bit. Try to speak in English with your family member as much as possible. It will not just improve your English, though it will improve their English too.
- Read English books of which you have watched the movies of – Readings books can be a little hard for ESOL, but not impossible. If you have watched a famous English movie, then it's easy for you to read its written version. But if you have not, then there are many famous books that have been made into movies you can watch and then read their books. Some of those famous movies are Titanic, Narnia, the Godfather, etc.
- Buy movies that have subtitles – Whether you buy DVDs or watch movies online, they should have the feature of the subtitle. Not all DVDs come with this feature, but it's clearly written whether it's got this feature or not on the cover. I'll recommend DVDs, because you can watch them again and again till you understand.
- Dialogue books – Read books with lots of dialogue. It will improve you speaking skills. Read different types of comics and focus on their dialogues.
- Read magazines – reading a magazine is one of the interesting

ways. It improves your understanding and knowledge about the ordinary or extraordinary people out there and helps you a lot.

- Join an English speaking course, if you can. It will improve your basic grammar skills in writing by which you'll be able to write, listen or read more effectively.
- Listen to English Radio – listening radio is one of the best English improving sources. Even though you don't understand English properly, it still does its job to improve you English. Keep your radio on all day and do your work.
- Learn English from games – One of the exciting ways of learning English is to play games that improve you, like brain trainer, brain challenge, brain age etc. If you don't have a game consoles, or emulators, then of course you would have at least a computer at home. You can play online brain training games on your computer.
- Watch English Cartoons shows – Watching cartoon shows on TV is interesting and effective way to improve English. Where you are taking the fun, there you're learning too. Watch shows with their English subtitles. Cartoon Network is one of the top cartoon channels and it has many cartoon shows that have subtitles included, so why not lift the advantages of them.
- Read children's books – Reading children's books improve your basic lacking, for example, do you know all the animals' name, fruits name, vegetables name, etc? No. If you feel like you deserve this level, then don't waste your time go ahead.
- Slangs and idioms – Learn slangs and idioms in English. People often use idioms or slangs when they speak. There are many websites over the internet, where you can find A to Z idioms. And there are many where you can find American slang terms. For example, urban dictionary, this offers you thousands of free slangs.
- Check how you sound like – Recording you voice in a recorder and check how you sound like. It tells you whether you sound good, or bad while speaking.

- Reference sites – If you don't have an electronic dictionary, still there is a key to know how the words are pronounced. Dictionary.com.
- Images for the word – also look for the images of the words you don't know. For example, if you are looking for the meaning of a word "wrapper", then search it on Google/images. Then later It will be easier for you to recognize the names of the things you come across.
- Travel a lot – Travel a lot. Find out places or things and do some research on things that look amazing and interesting to you and write your opinion about them. You need a blog to share your day by day tasks and journeys that you make.
- Learners of English must listen to each sentence in conversations (thematic dialogues) in audio materials several times and see their transcripts at the same time, and understand everything in those sentences clearly.
- It is necessary that learners of English read (pronounce) each sentence aloud and compare their pronunciation to the narrator's pronunciation.
- Speaking activity with self-control. It is essential for learners to check if they can orally convey the content of those dialogues closely to the original dialogues as much as possible. That means they must try to be an actor for both speakers in the dialogues. The most important thing for them is to speak English, and to check in the transcript of conversations (dialogues) whether they have made any mistakes in speaking.

  Learners can also make their own written questions on the dialogues that require long answers contained in the dialogues to facilitate (make easier) imitation of the dialogues. Alternatively, learners can write key words and phrases, or main ideas as a plan to make easier for them to imitate those dialogues.
- It is important that learners prepare potential questions and answers with important content on all everyday topics, and

practise speaking. To show different ways of expressing a particular thought they can make several potential questions and answers on one point in this speaking activity. There are two websites that contain a lot of ready-made questions in English on a wide variety of topics.

- Learners of English must have lists of difficult word meanings and of phrases (expressions) on every topic with usage sentences. They must read those ready-made vocabulary usage sentences many times if needed. Longman Language Activator Dictionary (unique English Idea Production Dictionary) covers this issue thoroughly. It is essential that learners also make their own sentences with that vocabulary, taking into consideration real life situations.
- Students of English can learn a lot of vocabulary on every topic from thematic English dictionaries. Good thematic English dictionaries provide clear word usage explanations and also a few usage sentences for each word meaning, which is especially important. It is essential that students of English also make their own sentences with difficult vocabulary. They should think about the real life situations where and when that vocabulary can be used.
- Learners can also master new English vocabulary by reading thematic texts (materials), first of all on everyday topics with important content, for example: Practical Tips and Advice to Make Everyday Life Easier and Better (practical solutions for everyday problems). Such self-help books on settling everyday matters are available at book stores.

  Learners must write down unknown vocabulary in whole sentences. It is essential that they practise telling the content of the texts that they have read. As people say, practice makes perfect.
- Constant review of material ensures solid knowledge and success in learning.
- It is very important that learners also make use of other important aids on a variety of topics to improve their English

conversation and vocabulary skills: audios, videos (English learning videos, travel videos, etc.), Internet resources, English learning magazines, newspapers, newsletters, radio programmes, TV programmes (educational programmes, documentary films, movies, news), books and e-books on a variety of subjects, online communication with native English speakers (chat, email, Skype).

- Good libraries have a wide selection of English learning aids.
- Observe the mouth movements of those who speak English well and try to imitate them.

  When you are watching television, observe the mouth movements of the speakers. Repeat what they are saying, while imitating the intonation and rhythm of their speech.
- Until you learn the correct intonation and rhythm of English, slow your speech down.

  If you speak too quickly, and with the wrong intonation and rhythm, native speakers will have a hard time understanding you.
- Don't worry about your listener getting impatient with your slow speech — it is more important that everything you say be understood.
- Use the dictionary.

  Try and familiarise yourself with the phonetic symbols of your dictionary. Look up the correct pronunciation of words that are hard for you to say.
- Make a list of frequently used words that you find difficult to pronounce and ask someone who speaks the language well to pronounce them for you.

  Record these words, listen to them and practice saying them. Listen and read at the same time.
- Buy books on tape.

  Record yourself reading some sections of the book. Compare

the sound of your English with that of the person reading the book on the tape.

- Pronounce the ending of each word.

  Pay special attention to 'S' and 'ED' endings. This will help you strengthen the mouth muscles that you use when you speak English.

- Read aloud in English for 15-20 minutes every day.

  Research has shown it takes about three months of daily practice to develop strong mouth muscles for speaking a new language.

- Record your own voice and listen for pronunciation mistakes.

  Many people hate to hear the sound of their voice and avoid listening to themselves speak. However, this is a very important exercise because doing it will help you become conscious of the mistakes you are making.

- Be patient.

  You can change the way you speak but it won't happen overnight. People often expect instant results and give up too soon. You can change the way you sound if you are willing to put some effort into it.

- Practice

  One of the best ways to improve your understanding of any language is to speak it as much as possible. Put yourself in situations where people speak primarily English, and try to keep up with the conversation. If you find yourself stuck on a word or confused by something a person says, do not be embarrassed to ask. Interacting with native English speakers on a regular basis will dramatically improve your ability to listen and speak.

- Enroll in a Class

  You truly want a firm grasp of the English language and its rules of grammar, syntax and usage, enroll in an English class. English is a complex language with many different pronunciations, grammatical constructions and spelling rules. Getting a grasp on these will advance your understanding of the language as well as your ability to read and write it. Stay positive in class, even when you feel challenged. Many native English speakers still have problems with some English words and spellings, such as the differences between "it's" and "its" and "there" and "their."

- Set Goals

  It is almost impossible to learn a language by studying it every now and then and hoping for results. Give yourself clear goals about how much you would like to learn, and in how much time. Breaking your language progress into clear, attainable goals will help you measure your progress as you go along. If you find yourself either falling behind your goals or accomplishing them with ease, adjust accordingly.

- Use the Media

  Sitting in classes, studying textbooks and trying to keep up with conversations can sometimes be frustrating. You can keep up with English in a more relaxed atmosphere by engrossing yourself in English media. This can include music, movies, television and books. Watching your favourite movie in English will help you build vocabulary and familiarize yourself with the language, and let you have fun in the process.

- Practise where you can, when you can. Any practice is good – whether you speak to someone who is a native English speaker or not.
- It's important to build your confidence. If possible, use simple English sentence structure that you know is correct, so that you can concentrate on getting your message across.
- Try to experiment with the English you know. Use words and phrases you know in new situations. Native English speakers are more likely to correct you if you use the wrong word than if you use the wrong grammar. Experimenting with vocabulary is a really good way of getting feedback.

- Try to respond to what people say to you. You can often get clues to what people think by looking at their body language. Respond to them in a natural way.
- Try not to translate into and from your own language. This takes too much time and will make you more hesitant.
- If you forget a word, do what native English speakers do all the time, and say things that 'fill' the conversation. This is better than keeping completely silent. Try using um, or er, if you forget the word.
- Don't speak too fast! It's important to use a natural rhythm when speaking English, but if you speak too fast it will be difficult for people to understand you.
- Try to relax when you speak.

  You'll find your mouth does most of the pronunciation work for you. When you speak English at normal speed, you'll discover that many of the pronunciation skills, such as linking between words, will happen automatically.
- Get a good dictionary.

  If you need to, a dictionary to translate between your first language and English is best.
- Practice every day by checking your pronunciation, and learning a few new words.
- Listen to people who speak English. If they talk too fast, kindly ask them to speak slower.
- Learn the grammar with careful study. A teacher may be best for this.
- Talk in English with other speakers, especially those who speak it as a first language.
- Think in English when you have learned it well.
- Translation in your brain can become confusing after certain points.
- Read Simple English in your spare time, such resources can

be found at the Simple English Wikipedia and books written for young children.

- Read aloud, so you are aware of how you speak.

  If you have English classes in school, listen and study as much as possible. The hard work will reward you with a master of the language.

Sample Dialogue in English

Srinath: Good morning, Sir. (greeting-formal)

Headmaster: Good morning Mr. Srinath.

Prabhu: Hello, Srinath. (greeting-informal)

Srinath: Hello Prabhu. how are you?

Prabhu: I'm fine. How are you?

Headmaster: I am glad you both have come on time.(expressing happiness)

Srinath: Sir, it is very kind of you to have invited us.(thanking-formal)

Headmaster: It's a pleasure! (responding to thanks) My wife suggested that we ask you both over to tea.

Prabhu: We too have been wanting to visit you.

Headmaster: Thanking you. (neutral)Shall we start with the slices of cake?(suggesting) Would you like these plum cakes?

Srinath: I would love to. (expressing liking)

Headmaster: Help yourselves with these sandwiches.(offering)

Prabhu: They are really delicious!

Headmaster: Mr. Sri, how do you like your tea? Strong (asking for liking)

Srinath: Not very strong Sir. Thank you. (thanking neutral)

Headmaster: Welcome! (responding to thanking you Mr. Prabhu?

Prabhu: A little strong, (stating slight preference)

Headmaster: I think you take more sugar.

Prabhu: Yes Sir, two spoonfuls.

Headmaster: Here you are. By the way, how's our students' performance?

Srinath: We can expect better result this year.

Headmaster: That's fine.

Prabhu: I can assure you a minimum of ten centums in Mathematics.

Headmaster: Oh, really. That's great! (expressing satisfaction) How about another cup of tea? (suggesting informal)

Prabhu: That's very kind of you. Sir (thanking- formal)\But I am afraid I am full. (refusing politely)

■■■

Chapter 3

Strategies for English Conversation

These strategies will help take your English communication skills to the next level. These points will help identify your weak points, learning style and learning goals while providing useful tips and steps to improve your English learning in class and at home.

How to Improve your English?

Learning English (or any language for that matter) is a process. You are continually improving your English and the following "How to" describes a strategy to make sure that you continue to improve effectively.

1. Remember that learning a language is a gradual process - it does not happen overnight.
2. Define your learning objectives early: What do you want to learn and why?
3. Make learning a habit. Try to learn something every day. It is much better to study (or read, or listen to English news, etc.) 10 minutes each day than to study for 2 hours once a week.
4. Remember to make learning a habit! If you study each day for 10 minutes English will be constantly in your head. If you study once a week, English will not be as present in your mind.

5 Choose your materials well. You will need reading, grammar, writing, speaking and listening materials

6. Vary your learning routine. It is best to do different things each day to help keep the various relationships between each area active. In other words, don't just study grammar.

7. Find friends to study and speak with. Learning English together can be very encouraging.

8. Choose listening and reading materials that relate to what you are interested in. Being interested in the subject will make learning more enjoyable - thus more effective.

9. Relate grammar to practical usage. Grammar by itself does not help you use the language.

10. Move your mouth! Understanding something doesn't mean the muscles of your mouth can produce the sounds. Practice speaking what you are learning aloud. It may seem strange, but it is very effective.

11. Be patient with yourself. Remember learning is a process - speaking a language well takes time. It is not a computer that is either on or off!

12. Communicate! There is nothing like communicating in English and being successful. Grammar exercises are good - having your friend on the other side of the world understand your email is fantastic!

13. Use the Internet. The Internet is the most exciting, unlimited English resource that anyone could imagine and it is right at your finger tips.

Tips

1. Remember that English learning is a process
2. Be patient with yourself
3. Practice, practice, practice

How to Improve your Pronunciation?

1. Learn the following rules concerning pronunciation.

2. English is considered a stressed language while many other languages are considered syllabic.
3. In other languages, such as French or Italian, each syllable receives equal importance (there is stress, but each syllable has its own length).
4. English pronunciation focuses on specific stressed words while quickly gliding over the other, non-stressed, words.
5. Stressed words are considered content words: Nouns e.g. kitchen, Paras – (most) principal verbs e.g. visit, construct – Adjectives e.g. beautiful, interesting - Adverbs often, carefully
6. Non-stressed words are considered function words: Determiners e.g. the, a – Auxiliary verbs e.g. am, were - Prepositions e.g. before, of – Conjunctions e.g. but, and - Pronouns e.g. they, she
7. Read the following sentence aloud: The beautiful Mountain appeared transfixed in the distance.
8. Read the following sentence aloud: He can come on Sundays as long as he doesn't have to do any homework in the evening.
9. Notice that the first sentence actually takes about the same time to speak well!
10. Even though the second sentence is approximately 30% longer than the first, the sentences take the same time to speak. This is because there are 5 stressed words in each sentence.
11. Write down a few sentences, or take a few example sentences from a book or exercise.
12. First underline the stressed words, then read aloud focusing on stressing the underlined words and gliding over the non-stressed words.
13. Be surprised at how quickly your pronunciation improves! By focusing on stressed words, non-stressed words and syllables take on their more muted nature.
14. When listening to native speakers, focus on how those speakers stress certain words and begin to copy this.

Tips:

1. Remember that non-stressed words and syllables are often 'swallowed' in English.
2. Always focus on pronouncing stressed words well, non-stressed words can be glided over.
3. Don't focus on pronouncing each word. Focus on the stressed words in each sentence.

Taking Tests

Doing well on English examinations - or any examination for that matter - depends not only on your knowledge, but also on having a good strategy.

1. Do not insist on completing each question before going to the next. By insisting on completing each question, you lose time and become nervous.
2. If possible, go through the entire test answering the questions you are sure you know.
3. Go through the test a second time working out the answers to more difficult questions.
4. Once you have gone through the test twice, see if any of the questions asked can help you answer any really difficult questions.
5. If you have a strong feeling about a question when you first answer it, don't go back and change it later.
6. Play the odds: If you don't know the answer, write something. In a 4 choice multiple choice question you have a 25% chance of being right.
7. Do not cheat! Taking a test is as much for you as it is for your teacher. If you cheat, you won't help yourself in the long run.
8. Do not translate from your mother tongue!
9. Don't block when listening.
10. Limit yourself to what you know.

11. Look for time signifiers when having to conjugate.
12. Throw out the ridiculous answers in a multiple choice question.
13. Don't try to b: too funny or clever.

Tips:

1. If you don't know an answer, don't worry about it. Worrying about what you don't know keeps you from showing what you do know.
2. Remember that tests not only given to test your ability, but also to help you learn what you need to focus on to improve your English.
3. If you don't understand why you have made a mistake, make sure to ask the teacher about that mistake in a latter session. Being embarrassed about mistakes will never help you improve, so ask!

Improving Vocabulary

There are many ways to improve your vocabulary. When working to improve your vocabulary it's important to know your goals in order to best choose the way in which you want to learn. Reading can be a great way to improve your vocabulary. However, it won't be much help on a vocabulary test next week. Here are a number of methods to help you improve, and expand, your English vocabulary.

1. Vocabulary Trees

   Vocabulary trees help provide context. Once you've mapped out a few vocabulary trees, you'll discover yourself thinking in vocabulary groups. When you see a cup your mind will quickly relate such words as knife, fork, late, dishes, etc. This overview to vocabulary trees provides will help you get started. Here is an example of a vocabulary tree.

2. Create Vocabulary Themes

   Create a list of vocabulary themes; include the vocabulary, a definition and an example sentence for each new item. Here is an example of a household appliance vocabulary theme sheet.

3. Use Technology to Help You

   Watching DVDs is a great way to help you understand native speakers of English. Using all the fancy options watching individual scenes can help make DVD use into a vocabulary learning exercise.

4. Specific Vocabulary Lists

   Rather than studying a long list of unrelated vocabulary, use specific vocabulary lists to help you prepare for the type of vocabulary you need for work, school or hobbies. These business vocabulary word lists are great for industry specific vocabulary items.

5. Visual Dictionaries

   A picture is worth a thousand words. It's also very helpful for learning precise vocabulary. There are a number of excellent English learner visual dictionaries for sale. Here is an online version of a visual dictionary dedicated to jobs.

6. Learn Collocations

   Collocations refer to words that often or always go together. A good example of a collocation is to do your homework. These lists of important verb + noun collocations will help your learn some of the most important.

7. Use a Corpus

   Corpora are huge collections of documents that can track the number of times a word is used. By using corpora, you can find which words are often used together with target vocabulary words. Combining corpora use with vocabulary trees is a great way to learn key vocabulary for specific vocabulary target areas. You can get started by visiting the British National Corpus.

Tips:

1. Use vocabulary learning methods to focus quickly on the vocabulary you need to study.
2. Don't make random lists of new words. Try to group words

in themes. This will help you memorize new words more quickly.

3. If you have the time, and even if you think you don't have the time, try to add context. Writing a few example sentences using new vocabulary will help you remember the words in context.
4. Keep a vocabulary notepad at hand whenever you are reading in English.

Intonation and Stress

Say this sentence aloud and count how many seconds it takes.

The beautiful Mountain appeared transfixed in the distance.

Time required? Probably about 5 seconds. Now, try speaking this sentence aloud.

He can come on Sundays as long as he doesn't have to do any homework in the evening.

Time required? Probably about 5 seconds.

Wait a minute the first sentence is much shorter than the second sentence!

The beautiful Mountain appeared transfixed in the distance.

He can come on Sundays as long as he doesn't have to do any homework in the evening

This simple exercise makes a very important point about how we speak and use English. Namely, English is considered a stressed language while many other languages are considered syllabic. What does that mean? It means that, in English, we give stress to certain words while other words are quickly spoken (some students say eaten!). In other languages, such as French or Italian, each syllable receives equal importance (there is stress, but each syllable has its own length).

Many speakers of syllabic languages don't understand why we quickly speak, or swallow, a number of words in a sentence. In syllabic languages each syllable has equal importance, and therefore equal time is needed. English however, spends more time on specific stressed words while quickly gliding over the other, less important, words

Let's look at a simple example: the modal verb "can". When we use the positive form of "can" we quickly glide over the can and it is hardly pronounced.

They can come on Friday. (Stressed words underlined)

On the other hand, when we use the negative form "can't" we tend to stress the fact that it is the negative form by also stressing "can't"?

They can't come on Friday.

As you can see from the above example the sentence, "They can't come on Friday" is longer than "They can come on Friday" because both the modal "can't" and the verb "come" are stressed.

So, what does this mean for my speaking skills?

Well, first of all, you need to understand which words we generally stress and which we do not stress. Basically, stress words are considered CONTENT WORDS such as

- Nouns e.g. kitchen, Paras
- (most) principal verbs e.g. visit, construct
- Adjectives e.g. beautiful, interesting
- Adverbs e.g. often, carefully

Non-stressed words are considered FUNCTION WORDS such as

- Determiners e.g. the, a, some, a few
- Auxiliary verbs e.g. don't, am, can, were
- Prepositions e.g. before, next to, opposite
- Conjunctions e.g. but, while, as
- Pronouns e.g. they, she, us

Let's return to the beginning example to demonstrate how this affects speech.

The beautiful Mountain appeared transfixed in the distance. (14 syllables)

He can come on Sunday s as long as he doesn't have to do any homework in the evening . (22 syllables)

Even though the second sentence is approximately 30% longer than the first, the sentences take the same time to speak. This is because there are 5 stressed words in each sentence. From this example, you can see that you needn't worry about pronouncing every word clearly to be understood (we native speakers certainly don't). You should however, concentrate on pronouncing the stressed words clearly.

Now, do some listening comprehension or go speak to your native English speaking friends and listen to how we concentrate on the stressed words rather than giving importance to each syllable. You will soon find that you can understand and communicate more because you begin to listen for (and use in speaking) stressed words. All those words that you thought you didn't understand are really not crucial for understanding the sense or making yourself understood. Stressed words are the key to excellent pronunciation and understanding of English.

Differences between American and British English

While there are certainly many more varieties of English, American and British English are the two varieties that are taught in most of the programmes. Generally, it is agreed that no one version is "correct" however, there are certainly preferences in use. The most important rule of thumb is to try to be consistent in your usage. If you decide that you want to use American English spellings then be consistent in your spelling (i.e. the colour of the orange is also its flavour - colour is American spelling and flavour is British), this is of course not always easy – or possible. The following guide is meant to point out the principal differences between these two varieties of English.

Use of the Present Perfect

In British English the present perfect is used to express an action that has occurred in the recent past that has an effect on the present moment. For example:

I've lost my key. Can you help me look for it?

In American English the following is also possible:

I lost my key. Can you help me look for it?

In British English the above would be considered incorrect. However, both forms are generally accepted in standard American English. Other differences involving the use of the present perfect in British English and simple past in American English include already, just and yet.

British English:

I've just had lunch

I've already seen that film

Have you finished your homework yet?

American English:

I just had lunch OR I've just had lunch.

I've already seen that film OR I already saw that film.

Have your finished your homework yet? OR Did you finish your homework yet?

Possession

There are two forms to express possession in English. Have or Have got

Do you have a car?

Have you got a car?

He hasn't got any friends.

He doesn't have any friends.

She has a beautiful new home.

She's got a beautiful new home.

While both forms are correct (and accepted in both British and American English), have got (have you got, he hasn't got, etc.) is generally the preferred form in British English while most speakers of American English employ the have (do you have, he doesn't have etc.)

The Verb Get

The past participle of the verb get is gotten in American English. Example He's gotten much better at playing tennis. British English – He's got much better at playing tennis.

Vocabulary

Probably the major differences between British and American English lies in the choice of vocabulary. Some words mean different things in the two varieties for example:

Mean: (American English – angry, bad humoured, British English – not generous, tight fisted)

Rubber: (American English – condom, British English – tool used to erase pencil markings)

There are many more examples. If there is a difference in usage, your dictionary will note the different meanings in its definition of the term. Many vocabulary items are also used in one form and not in the other. One of the best examples of this is the terminology used for automobiles.

- American English – hood

  British English – bonnet
- American English – trunk

  British English – boot
- American English – truck

  British English – lorry

Once again, your dictionary should list whether the term is used in British English or American English.

For a more complete list of the vocabulary differences between

British and American English use this British vs. American English vocabulary tool.

Prepositions

There are also a few differences in preposition use including the following:

- American English – on the weekend

  British English – at the weekend
- American English – on a team

  British English – in a team
- American English – please write me soon

  British English – please write to me soon

Past Simple/Past Participles

The following verbs have two acceptable forms of the past simple/past participle in both American and British English, however, the irregular form is generally more common in British English (the first form of the two) and the regular form is more common to American English.

- Burn

  Burnt OR burned
- Dream

  dreamt OR dreamed
- Lean

  leant OR leaned
- Learn

  learnt OR learned
- Smell

  smelt OR smelled
- Spell

  spelt OR spelled

- Spill

  spilt OR spilled

  Spoil

  spoilt OR spoiled

Spelling

Here are some general differences between British and American spellings:

Words ending in -or (American) -our (British) colour, colour, humour, humour, flavour, flavour etc.

Words ending in -ize (American) -ise (British) recognize, recognise, patronize, patronise etc.

The best way to make sure that you are being consistent in your spelling is to use the spell check on your word processor (if you are using the computer of course) and choose which variety of English you would like. As you can see, there are really very few differences between standard British English and standard American English. However, the largest difference is probably that of the choice of vocabulary and pronunciation.

■■■

Chapter 4

Small Talks

Small talk is used at parties, when meeting people, etc. to be kind and get along with others at the events. Hopefully, small talk leads to more interesting conversations. However, the ability to small talk and use appropriate phrases can help get the conversation flowing.

First Name, Last Name or Title?

Talking TO People

There are different ways to talk to people depending on your relationship and the situation. Here are the basics of using first name, titles, and other forms in spoken English.

First Name Only

Use the first name in informal and friendly situations. Use first name with your friends, co-workers, acquaintances and fellow students.

Hi, Vivek. Do you want to go to a film tonight? – Man to his friend.

Excuse me, Madhu. What did you think of that presentation yesterday? – Woman to a co-worker in the office.

Do you know the answer to number seven, Jimmy? – Student to another student.

If you are speaking with co-workers in the office about work, use a first name. However, if you are speaking to a supervisor or someone you manage, you may have to use a title and last name in more formal situations. The use of first name or title depends on the atmosphere in the office. Traditional businesses (banks, insurance companies, etc.) tend to be more formal. Young companies, such as internet companies, are often very informal.

Mr. Suresh, could you come to the meeting this afternoon? – Supervisor speaking to a subordinate at work.

Here is the report you asked for Mr. Jimmy. – Man to his supervisor.

Title and Last Name

Use the title (Mr, Mrs, Ms, etc.) and last name in formal situations such as meetings, public speaking, or when speaking to superiors at work or school. Remember that some work places prefer an informal tone between management and staff. It's best to begin using a title and last name (Hello, Ms Sharma!) and change if your supervisors ask you to use a first name basis.

Good morning Ms Arora. Did you have a good weekend? - Student to her teacher

Mr Arora, I'd like to introduce you to Jatin Verma from Delhi. – Employee introducing a colleague to his supervisor.

Talking ABOUT People

Speaking about other people also depends on the situation. Generally, in informal situations use first names. In more formal situations, use the title and last names. In addition to these choices, there are a few other possibilities.

First Name Only

Used in informal situations with friends and co-workers.

Have you heard that Madhu is moving to Los Angeles? – Boy speaking to his friend.

Pritam getting a promotion next month. – Woman speaking to a co-worker.

Last Name Only

When speaking about public figures such as actors and politicians, it is also quite common to use just the last name.

Bush is finally leaving soon! – One man to another.

Nadal is a monster on the court. – A tennis player speaking to his doubles partner.

Sometimes, supervisors might use just the last name when speaking to a co-worker.

Generally, this means the supervisor is not too happy.

Rahul hasn't completed the report on time. – Boss complaining to another manager.

Ask Naresh to come into the office as soon as he gets in. – Supervisor speaking to a co-worker.

First and Last Name

Use both the first and last name in informal and formal situations in order to be more specific in identifying a person.

Jitender Kumar was promoted to department head last week. – One co-worker to another.

Isn't that Susan Hart over there? – One friend to another.

Title and Last Name

Use the title and last name in more formal situations. Use this form when showing respect and / or being polite.

I think Ms Wright assigned some homework. - One student to a teacher.

I think Mr Ashok is the best candidate. – One voter speaking to another voter at a rally.

Introductions – Social Language

There are a number of phrases that are commonly used to introduce strangers.

(name), I don't think you've met (name).

I don't think you know (name)

May I introduce you to (name)

(name), do you know (name)?

(name), I'd like you to meet (name)

When you meet someone the first time, it is common to greet the person with "How do you do?" the correct response is "How do you do." Here is a short introductory conversation:

Karan: Paras, I'd like you to meet Madhu.

Paras: How do you do?

Madhu: How do you do.

Karan: Madhu works for ...

A variation is also "It's a pleasure to meet you." or "Pleased to meet you."

Karan: Paras, I'd like you to meet Madhu.

Paras: It's a pleasure to meet you.

Madhu: How do you do.

Paras: I'm great! So, what brought you here?

Greetings - Social Language

Once you have been introduced to someone, the next time you see that person it is important to greet them. We also greet people as we leave people. In English (as in all languages), there are different ways to greet people in formal and informal situations.

Formal Greeting are you?

Good day Sir / Madam (very formal)

Informal Greetings: Arriving

Hi / Hello

How are you?

What's up? (very informal)

How are you doing? (very informal)

It's important to note that the question "How are you?" or "What's up?" doesn't necessary need a response. If you do respond, these phrases are generally expected:

Very well, thank you. And you? (formal)

Fine / Great (informal)

Formal Greetings: Departing

Good morning / afternoon / evening.

It was a pleasure seeing you.

Goodbye.

Note: After 8 p.m. - Good night.

Informal Greetings: Departing

Goodbye / Bye.

See you (later).

Later (very informal

Special Days – Social Language

It is common to use a special greeting used just for that occasion on special days, holidays and other special occasions. Here are some of the most common:

Birthdays

Happy birthday!

Best wishes / Good luck on your thirtieth (age – use an ordinal number) birthday!

Many happy returns!

Wedding / Anniversary

Congratulations!

Best wishes / good luck on your tenth (number – use an ordinal number) anniversary!

Here's to many more happy years together (used when making a toast)

Special Holidays

Merry Christmas!

Happy New Year / Easter / Holi / Ramadan etc.

All the best for a happy New Year / Easter / Holi / Ramadan etc.

When making special greetings to children on their birthday and at Christmas, it is also common to ask them what they received:

Merry Christmas! What did you get from Santa Claus?

Happy Birthday! What did your Daddy get for you?

Special Occasions

Congratulations on your promotion!

All the best for your ...

I'm so proud of you!

Speaking to Strangers – Social Language

Here are a number of polite phrases used when trying to get the attention or help from people. The use of more formal language is common when speaking to someone you do not know:

Interrupting

It is common to first apologise before interrupting another person, or asking for help if you do not know the person.

Excuse me, could I ...

Sorry, do you think I could ...

Excuse me, do you know ...

I beg your pardon, could you help me? (formal)

Asking Someone to Repeat

When asking for information you may have a hard time

understanding in public places which can be very noisy (train stations, restaurants, stores, etc.). Here are phrases commonly used to ask someone to repeat what he has said:

Excuse me, I'm afraid I didn't understand. Could you repeat that? (formal)

I'm sorry, I didn't catch that. (informal)

What? (very informal!)

I beg your pardon.

Travel Greetings – Social Language

Here are a number of phrases used when saying goodbye to friends or family as they depart on trips, both short and long.

Long Trips, Vacations, etc. American English

Have a good trip.

Enjoy your vacation.

Have a good time in (destination)

Long Trips, Vacations, etc. British English

Have a good journey.

Enjoy your holidays.

Have a good time in (destination)

Short Outings

Enjoy! (American English)

Have a good time at (destination place such as a restaurant)

Have a good time in (destination city)

When your friends or family return home it is common to use one of the following phrases:

How was your vacation? (holiday in British English)

Did you enjoy your time in (destination)

How was your journey / flight / trip?

Starting a Conversation – Top Ten Questions

Here are ten questions to help you start speaking English. Each of these questions helps to begin or continue a conversation. The questions are in two categories: Basic Facts and Hobbies / Free Time. There are also a number of questions that can help you continue the conversation after the first question.

Five Basic Facts

These five questions will help you get to know people. They are simple questions with simple answers and provide information so you can ask more questions.

What is your name?

Where do you live?

What do you do?

Are you married?

Where are you from?

More questions for ...

These questions help to continue the conversation after your first question.

"What is your name?"

It's a pleasure to meet you. Where are you from?

That's an interesting name. Is it Chinese / French / Indian, etc.?

"Where do you live?"

How long have you lived there?

Do you like that neighbourhood?

Do you live in an apartment or house?

"What do you do?"

Which company do you work for?

How long have you had that job?

Do you like your job?

What's the best / worst thing about your job?

What do you like best / least about your job?

"Are you married?"

How long have been married?

Where did you get married?

What does your husband / wife do?

Do you have any children?

"Where are you from?"

Where is ....?

How long did you live there?

What is XYZ like?

Do you like living here?

Hobbies / Free Time

These questions will help you continue conversations and find out more about people's likes and dislikes.

What do you like doing in your free time?

Can you play tennis / golf / soccer / etc.?

What kind of films / food / vacations do you enjoy?

What do you do on weekends / Saturdays?

More questions for ...

These questions will help you ask for more detail.

"What do you like doing in your free time?"

How often do you (listen to music, eat out in restaurants, etc.)?

Where do you (listen to music, eat out in restaurants, etc.) in this town?

Why do you like (listening to music, eating out in restaurants, etc.) so much?

"Can you play tennis / golf / soccer / etc.?"

Do you enjoy playing tennis /golf /soccer /etc.?

How long have you played tennis /golf /soccer /etc.?

Who do you play tennis /golf /soccer /etc: with?

"What kind of films / food / vacations do you enjoy?"

What's the best place to see /eat / go on vacations?

What's the best type of film /food / vacation, etc. in your opinion?

How often do you watch films / eat out / go on vacation?

"What do you do on weekends / Saturdays?"

Where do you go to ...?

Could you recommend a good place to (go shopping / take my children swimming / etc.)?

How long have you done that?

Offering Help

There are a number of formulas used when offering help in English. Here are some of the most common:

- May I help you?
- Can I help you?
- Are you looking for something?
- Would you like some help?
- Do you need some help?
- What can I do for you today?

After you study these constructions, take the offering help quiz to check your understanding.

More English Functions

Disagreeing

Contrasting Ideas

Making Complaints

Asking for Information

Giving Advice

Guessing

Being Imprecise or Vague

Saying 'No' Nicely

Showing Preferences

Making Suggestions

Offering Help

Giving Warning

Demanding Explanations

Construction

Formula Verb Form

May I help you?

Use 'May I' or 'Can I' the base form of the verb in a statement.

Are you looking for something?

Use 'Are you looking for' something **OR** anything in particular OR specific object

Would you like some help?

Use 'Would you like' some help **OR some** advice OR a recommendation.

Do you need some help?

Use 'Do you need' some help OR some **advice** OR a recommendation.

What can I do for you today?

Use 'What can I do for' you, her, him, etc. today OR this morning, this afternoon, this evening.

Making Small Talk

The ability to make 'small talk' is highly valued. In fact, many English students are more interested in making effective small talk than knowing correct grammar structures – and rightly so! Small talk gets friendships started and 'breaks the ice' before important business meetings and other events.

What is small talk?

Small talk is pleasant conversation about common interests.

Why is small talk difficult for some English learners?

First of all, making small talk is not difficult only for English learners, but also for many native speakers of English. However, small talk can be especially difficult for some learners because making small talk means talking about almost anything – and that means having a wide vocabulary that can cover most topics. Most English learners have excellent vocabulary in specific areas, but may have difficulties discussing topics they are unfamiliar with because of a lack of appropriate vocabulary.

This lack of vocabulary leads to some students 'blocking'. They slow down or stop speaking completely because of a lack of self-confidence.

How to Improve Small Talk Skills?

Now that we understand the problem, the next step is to improve the situation. Here are some tips to improve small talk skills. Of course, making effective small talk means lots of practice, but keeping these tips in mind should improve overall conversational skills.

• Do some research.

Spend time on the Internet, reading magazines, or watching TV specials about the type of people you are going to meet. For example: If you are taking a class with students from other countries, take time after the first few days of class to do some research. They will appreciate your interest and your conversations will be much more interesting.

- Stay away from religion/strong political beliefs.

  While you may believe in something very strongly, beginning conversations and making small talk about your own personal convictions may abruptly end the conversation. Keep it light, don't try to convince the other person that you have the 'correct' information about a higher being, political system or other belief system.

- Use the Internet to gain specific vocabulary.

  This is related to doing research about other people. If you have a business meeting, or are meeting people who share a common interest (a basketball team, a tour group interested in art, etc.), take advantage of the Internet to learn specific vocabulary. Almost all businesses and interest groups have glossaries on the Internet explaining the most important jargon related to their business or activity.

- Ask yourself about your culture.

  Take time to make a list of common interests that are discussed when making small talk in your own culture. You can do this in your own language, but check to make sure that you have the English vocabulary to make small talk about those subjects.

- Find common interests.

  Once you have a subject that interests both of you, keep to it! You can do this in a number of ways: talking about travel, talking about the school or friend you have in common, talking about the differences between your culture and the new culture (just be careful to make comparisons and not judgements, i.e., The food in our country is better than the food here in England").

- Listen

  This is very important. Don't get so worried about being able to communicate that you don't listen. Listening carefully will help you understand and encourage those speaking to you. You might be nervous, but letting others state their opinions will improve the quality of the discussion - and give you time to think of an answer!

Demanding Explanations

Sometimes, things happen that we would like explained and we must demand explanations.

For example, if you have just bought a new computer and there is a problem, but the shop assistant says that the guaranty does not cover the problem. There are a number of formulas used when demanding explanations in English. Here are some of the most common:

- Can you tell me why...
- I don't understand why...
- Can you explain why..
- Why is it that...
- How come...
- Does this mean...
- Do you really expect me to believe...

After you study these constructions, take the demanding explanations quiz to check your understanding.

Construction

Formula Verb Form

Can you tell me why it has taken you so long to respond?

Use 'Can you tell me why' a full clause in the positive statement form (S V O). Notice that this is an indirect question and requires a question mark (?).

I don't understand why it has taken you so long to respond.

Use 'I don't understand why' a full clause in the positive statement form (S V O).

Notice that this is a statement and does NOT require a question mark (?)

Can you explain why it has taken you so long to respond?

Use 'Can you explain why' a full clause in the positive statement form (S V O). Notice that this is an indirect question and requires a question mark (?).

Why is it that it has taken you so long to respond?

Use 'Why is it that' a full clause in the positive statement form (S V O). Notice that this is an indirect question and requires a question mark (?).

How come it has taken you so long to respond?

Use 'How come' a full clause in the positive statement form (S V O). Notice that this is an indirect question and requires a question mark (?).

Does this mean (that) it has taken you so long to respond?

Use 'Does this mean (that)' a full clause in the positive statement form (S V O). Notice that this is an indirect question and requires a question mark (?).

Do you (really) expect me to believe (that) you weren't able to finish on time?

Use 'Do you (really) expect me to believe (that)' a full clause in the positive statement form (S V O). Notice that this is an indirect question and requires a question mark (?).

Using Vague Expressions – Being Imprecise

There are a number of ways to give imprecise information in English. Here are some of the most common:

- There are about 600 people working in this company.
- There are approximately 600 people working in this company.
- There are a large number of students interested in taking his course.

- Management predicts up to 50% growth for the coming year.
- It's kind of a bottle opener which can also be used to peel vegetables.
- It's the type of place you can go to relax for a week or so.
- They're the sort of people that like going bowling on Saturday evenings.
- It's difficult to say, but I'd guess that it's used for cleaning house.
- I'm not really sure, but I think they enjoy hiking in the mountains.

After you study these constructions, take the being imprecise or vague quiz to check your understanding.

More English Functions

Disagreeing	Contrasting Ideas
Making Complaints	Asking for Information
Giving Advice	Guessing
Being Imprecise or Vague	Saying 'No' Nicely
Showing Preferences	Making Suggestions
Offering Help	Giving Warning
Demanding Explanations	Construction

Formula Form

There are about 600 people working in this company. Use 'about' + a numbered expression.

There are approximately 600 people working in this company. Use 'approximately' + a numbered expression.

There are a large number of students interested in taking his course. Use 'a large number

of' + a noun.

Management predicts up to 50% growth for the coming year. Use 'up to' + a noun.

It's kind of a bottle opener which can also be used to peel vegetables. Use 'kind of' + a noun.

It's the type of place you can go to relax for a week or so. Use 'type of' + a noun. Use 'or so' at the end of a sentence to express the meaning 'approximately'.

They're the sort of people that like going bowling on Saturday evenings. Use 'sort of' + a noun.

It's difficult to say, but I'd guess that it's used for cleaning house. Use the phrase + 'It's difficult to say, but I'd guess' an independent clause.

Asking for Information

There are a number of formulas used when asking for information in English. Here are some of the most common:

- Could you tell me...?
- Do you know...?
- Do you happen to know...?
- I'd like to know...
- Could you find out...?
- I'm interested in...
- I'm looking for..

These two forms are used for asking for information on the telephone:

- I'm calling to find out...
- I'm calling about...

Apologising in English

It's common to use 'Excuse me, ...' before interrupting someone to ask for something in English. Another, more formal form is 'I beg your pardon ...'

Example Dialogues

Person 1: Excuse me, do you know what time it is?

Person 2: Yes, it's two o'clock.

Person 1: I beg your pardon. Would you minding helping me a moment?

Person 2: Certainly. What can I do to help?

In these cases, people are asking for help but begin the conversation by apologising. If you would like to apologise for something that you have done wrong, or misunderstood, the following phrases are appropriate:

I'm very sorry for / that ...

I apologise if I ...

I apologise for (+ ing form of verb)

Example Dialogues

Person 1: I'm very sorry for stepping on your foot!

Person 2: Don't worry about it. It's very crowded on this train.

Person 1: I apologise for my mistakes on this quiz.

Person 2: That's why you take quizzes - to learn!

Asking for Things

It's common to ask for things using yes / no polite phrases with 'Could you ...' and verbs such as 'lend', 'hand' and 'give'. Do not begin a sentence with 'please', but you can add 'please' at the end of the sentence to be polite.

NOT Please give me a pen

Correct: Could you give me a pen, please?

Example Dialogues

Person 1: Could you hand me that magazine?

Person 2: Certainly, here it is.

Person 1: Could you lend me a few dollars for lunch, please?

Person 2: I'd be happy to do that. How much do you need?

You can also ask for things using 'Could I ...' with verbs such as 'borrow', 'have', and 'use'.

Example Dialogues

Person 1: Could I borrow your pen, please?

Person 2: Certainly, here you are.

Person 1: Could I use that book?

Person 2: The red one, or the blue one?

Person 1: The blue one. Thank you.

It's also possible to ask for things more politely by using an indirect question.

Indirect questions begin with phrase such as 'Do you think ...', 'I wonder ...', 'Would it be alright if ...', etc.

Example Dialogues

Person 1: Would you mind loaning me your pen?

Person 2: Certainly, here you are.

Person 1: I wonder if you could help me with this problem?

Person 2: I'd be happy to do that. What seems to be the problem?

Asking People to Repeat

Sometimes, it is important to understand each piece of information when writing down a telephone number, or taking notes. Here are some phrases which you can use to ask people to repeat:

Would you mind repeating that?

Could I read that back to you?

Let me repeat that to double-check.

Example Dialogues

Person 1: The telephone number is 983 466-3978 983 466-3978

Person 2: Let me repeat the number to double-check. 983 466-3978 983 466-3978

Person 1: First, go down 3rd Ave to Black Street. Take a left, and continue on until you reach Harbour Blvd.

Person 2: Would you mind repeating that?

If you are at a party, or some other place where noise may interfere with your understanding, it's common to raise your voice a little and use one of the following phrases:

I'm sorry, I didn't catch (your name, the address, the name of the restaurant, etc).

Could you repeat that?

I'm having a problem understanding you. What's that again? (This phrase is also used on the telephone)

Example Dialogues

Person 1: Hi, my name is Paras. What's your name?

Person 2: Hi, I'm sorry, I didn't catch your name.

Person 1: It's a beautiful day today, isn't it?

Person 2: I'm having a problem understanding you. What's that again?

Expressing Sympathy

Sometimes bad things happen. When we hear about bad things that happen to other people it's a good idea to express sympathy. This can be difficult as we want to express our concern, but don't want to be intrusive. Here are some common phrases to help you express sympathy.

I'm sorry to hear about ...

Please accept my condolences. (Used when someone close to another has died)

That's so sad.

I hope things get better soon.

I hope you feel better soon.

Example Dialogues

Person 1: I've been rather sick lately.

Person 2: I hope you feel better soon.

Person 1: Tim has been having a lot of troubles lately. I think he might be getting a divorce.

Person 2: I'm sorry to hear about Tim's problems. I hope things get better for him soon.

It's also common to express sympathy in writing. Here are some common phrases you can use when writing a sympathy note to someone. Notice that is common to use the plural 'we' and 'our' when expressing written sympathy as a way to express that a family

My heartfelt condolences on your loss.

Our thoughts are with you.

She/he was a lot of things to many people and will be missed tremendously.

Thinking of you in your time of loss.

We are very saddened to hear of your loss. With deepest sympathies.

You have my sincere sympathy.

You have our deepest sympathy.

Getting People's Attention

It's common to use 'Excuse me, ...' to get someone's attention in English. Another, more formal form is 'I beg your pardon ...'

Example Dialogues

Person 1: Excuse me, do you know what time it is?

Person 2: Yes, it's two o'clock.

Person 1: I beg your pardon. Would you minding helping me a moment?

Person 2: Certainly. What can I do to help?

Sometimes, if a situation is more urgent, we use forms that might be considered rude in other less urgent situations. The most common of these forms is the imperative. The imperative form is also commonly used to give directions or commands, but in a dangerous situation can be used to warn.

Verb + Objects + !

Watch out!

Be careful!

Pay attention to what you are doing!

Going to Bed / Getting Up

Before we go to bed and when we get up in the morning it's common to make small talk about sleeping. Here are the most common phrases used:

Before Going to Bed

Good night.

Sleep well.

Have a good night's sleep.

Make sure to get a good night's sleep.

I hope you sleep well.

See you in the morning

Example Dialogues

Person 1: Good night.

Person 2: See you in the morning.

Person 1: I hope you sleep well.

Person 2: Thank you. Make sure you get a good night's sleep as well.

In the Morning, after Getting Up

I hope you had a good night's sleep.

Did you sleep well?

Did you have a good night's sleep?

I slept well, how about you?

Good morning. Did you sleep well?

How did you sleep?

Example Dialogues

Person 1: Good morning.

Person 2: Good morning. Did you sleep well?

Person 1: I hope you had a good night's sleep.

Person 2: Yes, thank you I did, and you?

Making Invitations

Inviting People

Inviting people to join you for dinner, social events, or other occasions is usually done using 'would like' to indicate the invitation. This form can be used for both formal and informal invitations. Remember that 'would you like ...' is always followed by the infinitive form of the verb (to do).

Example Dialogues

Person 1: Would you like to join us for dinner this evening?

Person 2: Thank you. Yes, that would be very nice.

Person 1: Would you like to come with us?

Person 2: Sure!

It's also common to use suggestion forms in more informal situations to invite other people to join you in doing something. These forms include 'let's do, how about / what about doing, shall we'.

Example Dialogues

Person 1: Let's go out on the town tonight.

Person 2: Yes, let's do that.

Person 1: Shall we get some dinner tonight?

Person 2: That sounds like fun.

Thanking People for Invitations

Always thank someone for inviting you to do something. Here are some of the most common forms used to accept an invitation.

Thank you very much.

That would be nice.

Certainly, I'd love to...

Sure, that would be great! (informal)

Example Dialogues

Person 1: Would you like to come over for dinner?

Person 2: That would be nice. Thank you.

Person 1: How about joining us for ice-cream?

Person 2: Sure, that would be great!

If you are unable to accept an invitation, use one of the following polite phrases to respond.

Thank you. I'm afraid I have another engagement.

Sorry, I'm afraid I can't.

Offering Something

It's common to use both 'would you like' and modal forms such as 'Can I ...', 'May I ...' to offer something. Here are some of the most important phrases used to offer something:

Can I get you some ...?

Would you like some ...?

May I offer you some ...?

Would you like me to get you some ....?

Example Dialogues

Person 1: Can I get you something to drink?

Person 2: Yes, that would be nice. Thank you.

Person 1: May I offer you some tea?

Person 2: Thank you.

Note: Always use 'some' words when offering someone something.

Accepting Offers

The following phrases are commonly used when accepting offers:

Thank you.

I'd love to.

I'd love some.

That would be nice.

Thank you. I'd like ...

Example Dialogues

Person 1: May I get you something to drink?

Person 2: Thank you. I'd like a cup of coffee.

Person 1: Would you like me to get you some food?

Person 2: That would be nice. Thank you.

Phrases used at Meals

Many languages use specific phrases before beginning a meal. Unfortunately, there are no traditional phrases used when beginning a meal. However, there are some phrases that are used during the meal, or by servers as they bring you your food.

At the Beginning of / During a Meal

This looks good / wonderful / tasty.

You've prepared a marvellous meal!

Yum, I can't wait to eat. (informal)

Server:

Enjoy your meal!

Example Dialogues

Person 1: You've prepared a marvellous meal! Thank you.

Person 2: I hope you like turkey!

Person 1: Enjoy your meal!

Person 2: Thank you.

At the End of a Meal

It's common to thank your host / cook at the end of a meal in a private home. Here are useful phrases to say thank you to the cook / host.

That was wonderful!

Thank you very much for such a great meal.

How did you prepare the ... it was wonderful!

Thank you so much for having us over for dinner.

Example Dialogues

Person 1: That was wonderful!

Person 2: I'm glad you enjoyed it.

Person 1: Thank you so much for having us over for dinner.

Person 2: It was our pleasure. We'll have to do it again.

Phrases used when Drinking

There are a number of phrases used when drinking at a bar or pub, or in a private home.

Here are some of the most common:

Cheers!

Here's to your health.

Bottoms up (informal, used with shots)

Example Dialogues

Person 1: Cheers!

Person 2: Bottoms up!

Person 1: Here's to your health.

Person 2: And to yours!

It's also common to use the phrase 'Here's to ...' or 'A toast to ...' and include the name of the person or thing you are toasting. In more formal occasions, we also use the phrase 'I'd like to make a toast to ...' and include the name of the person or thing you are toasting, as well as include a wish beginning with 'May he /she / it ...'.

Example Dialogues

Person 1: Here's to our new contract!

Person 2: Here, here!

Person 1: A toast to Manu!

Person 2: Cheers!

Person 1: I'd like to make a toast to Jimmy. May he live long and prosper!

Person 2: May he live long and prosper!

Asking Polite Questions

There are three main types of questions. Each of these question types can be used to form polite questions. Here's a quick overview of the three types of questions in English:

Direct Question

Where do you work?

Are they coming to the party?

How long has she worked for this company?

Indirect Question

Can you tell me where he plays tennis?

I wonder if you know what time it is.

Do you think she will be able to come next week?

Question Tags

You live in New York, don't you?

She hasn't studied French, has she?

We're good friends, aren't we?

Direct and indirect questions are used to ask about information you do not know. Question tags are generally used to check information you think you know.

Making Direct Questions Polite

Direct questions can seem impolite at times, especially when you are asking a stranger. For example, if you come up to someone and ask:

Does the tram stop here?

What time is it?

Can you move?

It is certainly correct to ask questions in this manner, but it's very common to make these types of questions more polite by adding 'excuse me' or 'pardon me' to begin your question.

Excuse me, when does the bus leave?

Excuse me, what time is it?

Pardon me, which form do I need?

Questions with 'can' are made more polite by using 'could':

Excuse me, could you help me pick this up?

Pardon me, could you help me?

Pardon me, could you give me a hand?

Another way of making direct questions more polite is to add 'please' at the end of the question:

Could you fill in this form, please?

Could you help me, please?

Can I have more soup, please?

NOT

Please, can I have more soup?

Indirect Questions: Very Polite

Using indirect question forms is an especially polite way of asking polite questions. The information requested is the same as in direct questions, but are considered more formal. Notice that an indirect question begins with a phrase (I wonder, Do you think, Would you mind, etc.) the actual question is then placed in positive sentence form:

Construction Chart

Introductory phrase + question word (or if) + positive sentence

I wonder if you could help me with this problem.

Do you know when the next train leaves?

Would you mind if I opened the window?

Note: If you are asking a 'yes - no' question use 'if' to connect the introductory phrase with the actual question statement. Otherwise, use a question word 'where, when, why, or how' to connect the two phrases.

Do you know if she will come to the party?

I wonder if you can answer a few questions.

Can you tell me if he is married?

CHAPTER 5

Commonly Used Words

Here is a list of the 1000 most common words in English. While this list is helpful for a strong beginning, more advanced vocabulary building will help you quickly improve your English.

Words from 1 to 250

1 the	2 of	3 to
4 and	5 a	6 in
7 is	8 it	9 you
10 that	11 he	12 was
13 for	14 on	15 are
16 with	17 as	18 I
19 his	20 they	21 be
22 at	23 one	24 have
25 this	26 from	27 or
28 had	29 by	30 hot
31 word	32 but	33 what
34 some	35 we	36 can

37 out	38 other	39 were
40 all	41 there	42 when
43 up	44 use	45 your
46 how	47 said	48 an
49 each	50 she	51 which
52 do	53 their	54 time
55 if	56 will	57 way
58 about	59 many	60 then
61 them	62 write	63 would
64 like	65 so	66 these
67 her	68 long	69 make
70 thing	71 see	72 him
73 two	74 has	75 look
76 more	77 day	78 could
79 go	80 come	81 did
82 number	83 sound	84 no
85 most	86 people	87 my
88 over	89 know	90 water
91 than	92 call	93 first
94 who	95 may	96 down
97 side	98 been	99 now
100 find	101 any	102 new
103 work	104 part	105 take
106 get	107 place	108 made
109 live	110 where	111 after
112 back	113 little	114 only
115 round	116 man	117 year

118 came	119 show	120 every
121 good	122 me	123 give
124 our	125 under	126 name
127 very	128 through	129 just
130 form	131 sentence	132 great
133 think	134 say	135 help
136 low	137 line	138 differ
139 turn	140 cause	141 much
142 mean	143 before	144 move
145 right	146 boy	147 old
148 too	149 same	150 tell
151 does	152 set	153 three
154 want	155 air	156 well
157 also	158 play	159 small
160 end	161 put	162 home
163 read	164 hand	165 port
166 large	167 spell	168 add
169 even	170 land	171 here
172 must	173 big	174 high
175 such	176 follow	177 act
178 why	179 ask	180 men
181 change	182 went	183 light
184 kind	185 off	186 need
187 house	188 picture	189 try
190 us	191 again	192 animal
193 point	194 mother	195 world
196 near	197 build	198 self

199 earth 200 father 201 head
202 stand 203 own 204 page
205 should 206 country 207 found
208 answer 209 school 210 grow
211 study 212 still 213 learn
214 plant 215 cover 216 food
217 sun 218 four 219 between
220 state 221 keep 222 eye
223 never 224 last 225 let
226 thought 227 city 228 tree
229 cross 230 farm 231 hard
232 start 233 might 234 story
235 saw 236 far 237 sea
238 draw 239 left 240 late
241 run 242 don't 243 while
244 press 245 close 246 night
247 real 248 life 249 few
250 north

Words from 250 to 500

251 open 252 seem 253 together
254 next 255 white 256 children
257 begin 258 got 259 walk
260 example 261 ease 262 paper
263 group 264 always 265 music
266 those 267 both 268 mark
269 often 270 letter 271 until
272 mile 273 river 274 car

275 feet	276 care	277 second
278 book	279 carry	280 took
281 science	282 eat	283 room
284 friend	285 began	286 idea
287 fish	288 mountain	289 stop
290 once	291 base	292 hear
293 horse	294 cut	295 sure
296 watch	297 colour	298 face
299 wood	300 main	301 enough
302 plain	303 girl	304 usual
305 young	306 ready	307 above
308 ever	309 red	310 list
311 though	312 feel	313 talk
314 bird	315 soon	316 body
317 dog	318 family	319 direct
320 pose	321 leave	322 song
323 measure	324 door	325 product
326 black	327 short	328 numeral
329 class	330 wind	331 question
332 happen	333 complete	334 ship
335 area	336 half	337 rock
338 order	339 fire	340 south
341 problem	342 piece	343 told
344 knew	345 pass	346 since
347 top	348 whole	349 king
350 space	351 heard	352 best
353 hour	354 better	355 true

356 during	357 hundred	358 five
359 remember	360 step	361 early
362 east	363 west	364 ground
365 interest	366 reach	367 fast
368 verb	369 sing	370 listen
371 six	372 table	373 travel
374 less	375 morning	376 ten
377 simple	378 several	379 vowel
380 toward	381 war	382 lay
383 against	384 pattern	385 slow
386 center	387 love	388 person
389 money	390 serve	391 appear
392 road	393 map	394 rain
395 rule	396 govern	397 pull
398 cold	399 notice	400 voice
401 unit	402 power	403 town
404 fine	405 certain	406 fly
407 fall	408 lead	409 cry
410 dark	411 machine	412 note
413 wait	414 plan	415 figure
416 star	417 box	418 noun
419 field	420 rest	421 correct
422 able	423 pound	424 done
425 beauty	426 drive	427 stood
428 contain	429 front	430 teach
431 week	432 final	433 gave
434 green	435 oh	436 quick

437 develop	438 ocean	439 warm
440 free	441 minute	442 strong
443 special	444 mind	445 behind
446 clear	447 tail	448 produce
449 fact	450 street	451 inch
452 multiply	453 nothing	454 course
455 stay	456 wheel	457 full
458 force	459 blue	460 object
461 decide	462 surface	463 deep
464 moon	465 island	466 foot
467 system	468 busy	469 test
470 record	471 boat	472 common
473 gold	474 possible	475 plane
476 stead	477 dry	478 wonder
479 laugh	480 thousand	481 ago
482 ran	483 check	484 game
485 shape	486 equate	487 hot
488 miss	489 brought	490 heat
491 snow	492 tire	493 bring
494 yes	495 distant	496 fill
497 east	498 paint	499 language
500 among		

Words from 500 to 750

501 grand	502 ball	503 yet
504 wave	505 drop	506 heart
507 am	508 present	509 heavy
510 dance	511 engine	512 position

513 arm
514 wide
515 sail
516 material
517 size
518 vary
519 settle
520 speak
521 weight
522 general
523 ice
524 matter
525 circle
526 pair
527 include
528 divide
529 syllable
530 felt
531 perhaps
532 pick
533 sudden
534 count
535 square
536 reason
537 length
538 represent
539 art
540 subject
541 region
542 energy
543 hunt
544 probable
545 bed
546 brother
547 egg
548 ride
549 cell
550 believe
551 fraction
552 forest
553 sit
554 race
555 window
556 store
557 summer
558 train
559 sleep
560 prove
561 lone
562 leg
563 exercise
564 wall
565 catch
566 mount
567 wish
568 sky
569 board
570 joy
571 winter
572 sat
573 written
574 wild
575 instrument
576 kept
577 glass
578 grass
579 cow
580 job
581 edge
582 sign
583 visit
584 past
585 soft
586 fun
587 bright
588 gas
589 weather
590 month
591 million
592 bear
593 finish

594 happy
595 hope
596 flower
597 clothe
598 strange
599 gone
600 jump
601 baby
602 eight
603 village
604 meet
605 root
606 buy
607 raise
608 solve
609 metal
610 whether
611 push
612 seven
613 paragraph
614 third
615 shall
616 held
617 hair
618 describe
619 cook
620 floor
621 either
622 result
623 burn
624 hill
625 safe
626 cats
627 century
628 consider
629 type
630 law
631 bit
632 coast
633 copy
634 phrase
635 silent
636 tall
637 sand
638 soil
639 roll
640 temperature
641 finger
642 industry
643 value
644 fight
645 lie
646 beat
647 excite
648 natural
649 view
650 sense
651 ear
652 else
653 quite
654 broke
655 case
656 middle
657 kill
658 son
659 lake
660 moment
661 scale
662 loud
663 spring
664 observe
665 child
666 straight
667 consonant
668 nation
669 dictionary
670 milk
671 speed
672 method
673 organ
674 pay

675 age
676 section
677 dress
678 cloud
679 surprise
680 quiet
681 stone
682 tiny
683 climb
684 cool
685 design
686 poor
687 lot
688 experiment
689 bottom
690 key
691 iron
692 single
693 stick
694 flat
695 twenty
696 skin
697 smile
698 crease
699 hole
700 trade
701 melody
702 trip
703 office
704 receive
705 row
706 mouth
707 exact
708 symbol
709 die
710 least
711 trouble
712 shout
713 except
714 wrote
715 seed
716 tone
717 join
718 suggest
719 clean
720 break
721 lady
722 yard
723 rise
724 bad
725 blow
726 oil
727 blood
728 touch
729 grew
730 cent
731 mix
732 team
733 wire
734 cost
735 lost
736 brown
737 wear
738 garden
739 equal
740 sent
741 choose
742 fell
743 fit
744 flow
745 fair
746 bank
747 collect
748 save
749 control
750 decimal

Words from 751 to 1000

751 gentle	752 woman	753 captain
754 practice	755 separate	756 difficult
757 doctor	758 please	759 protect
760 noon	761 whose	762 locate
763 ring	764 character	765 insect
766 caught	767 period	768 indicate
769 radio	770 spoke	771 atom
772 human	773 history	774 effect
775 electric	776 expect	777 crop
778 modern	779 element	780 hit
781 student	782 corner	783 party
784 supply	785 bone	786 rail
787 imagine	788 provide	789 agree
790 thus	791 capital	792 won't
793 chair	794 danger	795 fruit
796 rich	797 thick	798 soldier
799 process	800 operate	801 guess
802 necessary	803 sharp	804 wing
805 create	806 neighbour	807 wash
808 bat	809 rather	810 crowd
811 corn	812 compare	813 poem
814 string	815 bell	816 depend
817 meat	818 rub	819 tube
820 famous	821 dollar	822 stream
823 fear	824 sight	825 thin

826 triangle
827 planet
828 hurry
829 chief
830 colony
831 clock
832 mine
833 tie
834 enter
835 major
836 fresh
837 search
838 send
839 yellow
840 gun
841 allow
842 print
843 dead
844 spot
845 desert
846 suit
847 current
848 lift
849 rose
850 continue
851 block
852 chart
853 hat
854 sell
855 success
856 company
857 subtract
858 event
859 particular
860 deal
861 swim
862 term
863 opposite
864 wife
865 shoe
866 shoulder
867 spread
868 arrange
869 camp
870 invent
871 cotton
872 born
873 determine
874 quart
875 nine
876 truck
877 noise
878 level
879 chance

Adjective or Adverb?

880 gather
881 shop
882 stretch
883 throw
884 shine
885 property
886 column
887 molecule
888 select
889 wrong
890 gray
891 repeat
892 require
893 broad
894 prepare
895 salt
896 nose
897 plural
898 anger
899 claim
900 continent
901 oxygen
902 sugar
903 death

904 pretty 905 skill 906 women
907 season 908 solution 909 magnet
910 silver 911 thank 912 branch
913 match 914 suffix 915 especially
916 fig 917 afraid 918 huge
919 sister 920 steel 921 discuss
922 forward 923 similar 924 guide
925 experience 926 score 927 apple
928 bought 929 led 930 pitch
931 coat 932 mass 933 card
934 band 935 rope 936 slip
937 win 938 dream 939 evening
940 condition 941 feed 942 tool
943 total 944 basic 945 smell
946 valley 947 nor 948 double
949 seat 950 arrive 951 master
952 track 953 parent 954 shore
955 division 956 sheet 957 substance
958 favour 959 connect 960 post
961 spend 962 chord 963 fat
964 glad 965 original 966 share
967 station 968 dad 969 bread
970 charge 971 proper 972 bar
973 offer 974 segment 975 slave
976 duck 977 instant 978 market
979 degree 980 populate 981 chick
982 dear 983 enemy 984 reply

985 drink	986 occur	987 support
988 speech	989 nature	990 range
991 steam	992 motion	993 path
994 liquid	995 log	996 meant
997 quotient	998 teeth	999 shell
1000 neck		

Top Most Uses of Nouns

Here is a list of most commonly used nouns along with suitable examples. Students intending to improve conversational skill through vocabulary should try to include them in their daily conversations.

age	The age of my daughter is three.
air	The air is quite clear today.
anger	His anger knows no limits.
animal	I'm not sure of the name of that animal over there in that cage.
answer	He provided an excellent answer to my question.
apple	I love a good red apple after dinner.
area	This area is intended for recreation
arm	He put his arm out for inspection.
art	It would be difficult to live without art.
atom	One of the smallest elements is the atom.
baby	She put her baby into its crib.
back	I turned my back on that outrageous man.
ball	He hit the ball out of the park.
band	The band played until three in the morning.
bank	The bank closes at three in the afternoon.
bar	Let's go to the bar and get a beer.

base	He works at the base on the other side of town.
bat	If you look up there you can see a bat flying between the trees.
bear	The bear is a dangerous but playful animal.
beauty	The countryside is splendid in its beauty.
bell	He rang the bell to signal the end of class.
bird	Do you know the name of that bird on that branch?
bit	Could you hand me that bit for this drill?
block	He picked up the block of wood and began to work on it.
blood	Look at the blood on the floor! What's happened?
blow	He received a mighty blow from his opponent in the boxing match.
board	Use that board over there to cover up the window.
boat	He bought a new boat for his birthday.
body	He left the body at the side of the road.
bone	I found a prehistoric bone in the desert.
book	You should read this book!
bottom	You will find the coin at the bottom of the lake.
box	I put the extra clothes into that box.
boy	Do you see that boy over there?
branch	There is a bird on that branch.
bread	Could you get some bread when you go to the market?
break	I'll take a five minute break and then get back to work.
brother	My brother lives in Gurgaon.
call	Give me a call when you arrive.

camp	I set up camp at the edge of the wood.
capital	The capital of Washington state is Olympia.
captain	The captain told his crew to raise the sail.
car	He drove his car very fast.
card	Let me give you my business card.
care	She received excellent care at the hospital.
case	You will find the bottle of wine in that case over there.
cat	My cat is four years old.
cause	I'm sure his lack of understanding was the cause of his failure.
cell	The cell is one of nature's wonders.
cent	If I had every cent I have wasted I would be a very rich man indeed.
century	Last century was at times horrific and at times marvellous.
chair	Let me get a chair and sit down.
chance	If you just give him a chance you will see how capable he really is.
change	I need a change in my life!
character	Her character can be very frustrating at times.
chick	He picked up the little chick that had just been born.
chief	Just a moment, I need to speak to the chief.
child	He gave the child a dime.
children	We have five children!
chord	The pianist played the marvellous chord.
circle	Draw a circle on a piece of paper and write your ideas in it.

city	Life in a city can be both wonderful and frustrating.
class	He came to class late.
climb	The climb to the top of the peak was challenging.
clock	We need a new clock for the living room.
cloud	The cloud appeared on the horizon and I knew it would rain soon.
coast	Let's go to the coast for the weekend.
coat	It's cold outside! Make sure to put your coat on.
cold	The cold in this room is unbearable.
colony	The British established the colony in 1876.
colour	That is it's true colour!
column	I read his latest column in the Times of India.
company	He's worked for that company for over five years.
condition	Has his condition improved?
consonant	That is a consonant that you don't have in your language.
continent	She lives on a different continent.
copy	Can you give me a copy of that report?
corn	This corn is so sweet! Where did you get it?
cost	You can buy a used car at a low cost.
cotton	Cotton is used to make many different types of clothes.
country	He lives in a country where free speech is not allowed.
course	I'm taking a computer course at the local college.
cover	The cover of this week's issue is really shocking.
cow	He has a cow that he milks every day.
crop	This year's crop was excellent.

cross	He hang a cross over his desk.
crowd	That crowd went wild at his last statement.
cry	Her cry could be heard above the crowd.
current	The current is really strong in that river.
cut	How did you get that cut?
dad	I visited my dad last week.
dance	Would you like to go to the dance with me this Saturday?
danger	There is great danger in those woods.
day	What a great day!
dead	Many people believe the dead come back to haunt.
deal	I made a deal with Rohit's.
death	His death disturbed her greatly.
decimal	The decimal was 5/6.
degree	He will soon receive his degree.
design	Her design won the best project of the year award.
dictionary	Look that up in the dictionary if you don't understand.
division	I work in the sales division.
doctor	You'd better see a doctor about that cough.
dog	My daughter would love to have a dog.
dollar	He paid top dollar for that car.
door	Let me open the door for you.
double	Double your money in 7 years.
draw	I lost the draw and so I have to go last.
dream	She same him clearly in her dream last night.
dress	She wore that pretty blue dress to the party.

drink	Would you like a drink? - Maybe a gin and tonic?
drive	The drive up to the canyon was beautiful.
drop	The drop was almost 500 metres straight down!
duck	Do you see that cute duck swimming over there?
ear	Lend me an ear and I will tell you an interesting story.
earth	He moved about two tons of earth this weekend.
ease	The ease with which he plays tennis shows how often he plays.
east	The east will always be different from the west.
edge	Be careful! Don't get too close to the edge!
effect	We still don't know the long term effect his actions will have.
egg	Would you like your egg boiled or fried?
eight	There are eight in the room.
element	One important element is hard study.
end	We are nearing the end of the journey.
enemy	His enemy attacked him.
energy	She has so much energy! Just think of all the different things she does.

Commonly Used Adjectives

Adjectives are used to add descriptions. Here is a list of some of the commonly used adjectives.

1. able	2. acidic	3. angry
4. automatic	5. awake	6. bad
7. beautiful	8. bent	9. bitter
10. black	11. blue	12. boiling
13. bright	14. broken	15. brown

16. certain
17. cheap
18. chemical
19. chief
20. clean
21. clear
22. cold
23. common
24. complete
25. complex
26. conscious
27. cruel
28. cut
29. dark
30. dead
31. dear
32. deep
33. delicate
34. dependent
35. different
36. dirty
37. dry
38. early
39. elastic
40. electric
41. equal
42. false
43. fat
44. feeble
45. female
46. fertile
47. first
48. fixed
49. flat
50. foolish
51. free
52. frequent
53. full
54. future
55. general
56. good
57. grey
58. great
59. green
60. hanging
61. happy
62. hard
63. healthy
64. high
65. hollow
66. ill
67. important
68. kind
69. last
70. late
71. left
72. like
73. living
74. long
75. loose
76. loud
77. low
78. male
79. married
80. material
81. medical
82. military
83. mixed
84. narrow
85. natural
86. necessary
87. new
88. normal
89. old
90. open
91. opposite
92. parallel
93. past
94. physical
95. political
96. poor

97. possible	98. present	99. private
100. probable	101. public	102. quick
103. quiet	104. ready	105. red
106. regular	107. responsible	108. right
109. rough	110. round	111. sad
112. safe	113. same	114. second
115. secret	116. separate	117. serious
118. sharp	119. short	120. shut
121. simple	122. slow	123. small
124. smooth	125. soft	126. solid
127. special	128. sticky	129. stiff
130. straight	131. strange	132. strong
133. sudden	134. sweet	135. tall
136. thick	137. thin	138. tight
139. tired	140. true	141. violent
142. waiting	143. warm	144. wet
145. white	146. wide	147. wise
148. wrong	149. yellow	150. young

Commonly Used Verbs, Prepositions, Articles, Pronouns, etc.

1. come	2. get	3. give
4. go	5. keep	6. let
7. make	8. put	9. seem
10. take	11. be	12. do
13. have	14. say	15. see
16. send	17. may	18. will
19. about	20. across	21. after

22. against
23. among
24. at
25. before
26. between
27. by
28. down
29. from
30. in
31. off
32. on
33. over
34. through
35. to
36. under
37. up
38. with
39. as
40. for
41. of
42. till
43. than
44. a
45. the
46. all
47. any
48. every
49. no
50. other
51. some
52. such
53. that
54. this
55. i
56. he
57. you
58. who
59. and
60. because
61. but
62. or
63. if
64. though
65. while
66. how
67. when
68. where
69. why
70. again
71. ever
72. far
73. forward
74. here
75. near
76. now
77. out
78. still
79. then
80. there
81. together
82. well
83. almost
84. enough
85. even
86. little
87. much
88. not
89. only
90. quite
91. so
92. very
93. tomorrow
94. yesterday
95. north
96. south
97. east
98. west
99. please
100. yes

Commonly Used General Nouns

1. account	2. act	3. addition
4. adjustment	5. advertisement	6. agreement
7. air	8. amount	9. amusement
10. animal	11. answer	12. apparatus
13. approval	14. argument	15. art
16. attack	17. attempt	18. attention
19. attraction	20. authority	21. back
22. balance	23. base	24. behaviour
25. belief	26. birth	27. bit
28. bite	29. blood	30. blow
31. body	32. brass	33. bread
34. breath	35. brother	36. building
37. burn	38. burst	39. business
40. butter	41. canvas	42. care
43. cause	44. chalk	45. chance
46. change	47. cloth	48. coal
49. colour	50. comfort	51. committee
52. company	53. comparison	54. competition
55. condition	56. connection	57. control
58. cook	59. copper	60. copy
61. cork	62. copy	63. cough
64. country	65. cover	66. crack
67. credit	68. crime	69. crush
70. cry	71. current	72. curve
73. damage	74. danger	75. daughter
76. day	77. death	78. debt

79. decision
80. degree
81. design
82. desire
83. destruction
84. detail
85. development
86. digestion
87. direction
88. discovery
89. discussion
90. disease
91. disgust
92. distance
93. distribution
94. division
95. doubt
96. drink
97. driving
98. dust
99. earth
100. edge
101. education
102. effect
103. end
104. error
105. event
106. example
107. exchange
108. existence
109. expansion
110. experience
111. expert
112. fact
113. fall
114. family
115. father
116. fear
117. feeling
118. fiction
119. field
120. fight
121. fire
122. flame
123. flight
124. flower
125. fold
126. food
127. force
128. form
129. friend
130. front
131. fruit
132. glass
133. gold
134. government
135. grain
136. grass
137. grip
138. group
139. growth
140. guide
141. harbour
142. harmony
143. hate
144. hearing
145. heat
146. help
147. history
148. hole
149. hope
150. hour
151. humour
152. ice
153. idea
154. impulse
155. increase
156. industry
157. ink
158. insect
159. instrument

160. insurance
161. interest
162. invention
163. iron
164. jelly
165. join
166. journey
167. judge
168. jump
169. kick
170. kiss
171. knowledge
172. land
173. language
174. laugh
175. low
176. lead
177. learning
178. leather
179. letter
180. level
181. lift
182. light
183. limit
184. linen
185. liquid
186. list
187. look
188. loss
189. love
190. machine
191. man
192. manager
193. mark
194. market
195. mass
196. meal
197. measure
198. meat
199. meeting
200. memory
201. metal
202. middle
203. milk
204. mind
205. mine
206. minute
207. mist
208. money
209. month
210. morning
211. mother
212. motion
213. mountain
214. move
215. music
216. name
217. nation
218. need
219. news
220. night
221. noise
222. note
223. number
224. observation
225. offer
226. oil
227. operation
228. opinion
229. order
230. organisation
231. ornament
232. owner
233. page
234. pain
235. paint
236. paper
237. part
238. paste
239. payment
240. peace

241. person
242. place
243. plant
244. play
245. pleasure
246. point
247. poison
248. polish
249. porter
250. position
251. powder
252. power
253. price
254. print
255. process
256. produce
257. profit
258. property
259. prose
260. protest
261. pull
262. punishment
263. purpose
264. push
265. quality
266. question
267. rain
268. range
269. rate
270. ray
271. reaction
272. reading
273. reason
274. record
275. regret
276. relation
277. religion
278. representative
279. request
280. respect
281. rest
282. reward
283. rhythm
284. rice
285. river
286. road
287. roll
288. room
289. rub
290. rule
291. run
292. salt
293. sand
294. scale
295. science
296. sea
297. seat
298. secretary
299. selection
300. self
301. sense
302. servant
303. sex
304. shade
305. shake
306. shame
307. shock
308. side
309. sign
310. silk
311. silver
312. sister
313. size
314. sky
315. sleep
316. slip
317. slope
318. smash
319. smell
320. smile
321. smoke

322. sneeze
323. snow
324. soap
325. society
326. son
327. song
328. sort
329. sound
330. soup
331. space
332. stage
333. start
334. statement
335. steam
336. steel
337. step
338. stitch
339. stone
340. stop
341. story
342. stretch
343. structure
344. substance
345. sugar
346. suggestion
347. summer
348. support
349. surprise
350. swim
351. system
352. talk
353. taste
354. tax
355. teaching
356. tendency
357. test
358. theory
359. thing
360. thought
361. thunder
362. time
363. tin
364. top
365. touch
366. trade
367. transport
368. trick
369. trouble
370. turn
371. twist
372. unit
373. use
374. value
375. verse
376. vessel
377. view
378. voice
379. walk
380. war
381. wash
382. waste
383. water
384. wave
385. wax
386. way
387. weather
388. week
389. weight
390. wind
391. wine
392. winter
393. woman
394. wood
395. wool
396. word
397. work
398. wound
399. writing
400. year

Commonly Used Specific Nouns

1. angle
2. ant
3. apple
4. arch
5. arm
6. army
7. baby
8. bag
9. ball
10. band
11. basin
12. basket
13. bath
14. bed
15. bee
16. bell
17. berry
18. bird
19. blade
20. board
21. boat
22. bone
23. book
24. boot
25. bottle
26. box
27. boy
28. brain
29. brake
30. branch
31. brick
32. bridge
33. brush
34. bucket
35. bulb
36. button
37. cake
38. camera
39. card
40. carriage
41. cart
42. cat
43. chain
44. cheese
45. chess
46. chin
47. church
48. circle
49. clock
50. cloud
51. coat
52. collar
53. comb
54. cord
55. cow
56. cup
57. curtain
58. cushion
59. dog
60. door
61. drain
62. drawer
63. dress
64. drop
65. ear
66. egg
67. engine
68. eye
69. face
70. farm
71. feather
72. finger
73. fish
74. flag
75. floor

76. fly	77. foot	78. fork
79. fowl	80. frame	81. garden
82. girl	83. glove	84. goat
85. gun	86. hair	87. hammer
88. hand	89. hat	90. head
91. heart	92. hook	93. horn
94. horse	95. hospital	96. house
97. island	98. jewel	99. kettle
100. key	101. knee	102. knife
103. knot	104. leaf	105. leg
106. library	107. line	108. lip
109. lock	110. map	111. match
112. monkey	113. moon	114. mouth
115. muscle	116. nail	117. neck
118. needle	119. nerve	120. net
121. nose	122. nut	123. office
124. orange	125. oven	126. parcel
127. pen	128. pencil	129. picture
130. pig	131. pin	132. pipe
133. plane	134. plate	135. plough
136. pocket	137. pot	138. potato
139. prison	140. pump	141. rail
142. rat	143. receipt	144. ring
145. rod	146. roof	147. root
148. sail	149. school	150. scissors
151. screw	152. seed	153. sheep

154. shelf
155. ship
156. shirt
157. shoe
158. skin
159. skirt
160. snake
161. sock
162. spade
163. sponge
164. spoon
165. spring
166. square
167. stamp
168. star
169. station
170. stem
171. stick
172. stocking
173. stomach
174. store
175. street
176. sun
177. table
178. tail
179. thread
180. throat
181. thumb
182. ticket
183. toe
184. tongue
185. tooth
186. town
187. train
188. tray
189. tree
190. trousers
191. umbrella
192. wall
193. watch
194. wheel
195. whip
196. whistle
197. window
198. wing
199. wire
200. worm

CHAPTER 6

Improving Vocabulary

Confusing Words

Here are some of the most commonly confused English word pairs.

beside / besides

beside: preposition meaning 'next to', 'at the side of'

Examples: I sit beside Sohan in class.

Could you get me that book? It's beside the lamp.

besides: adverb meaning 'also', 'as well'; preposition meaning 'in addition to'

Examples: (adverb) He's responsible for sales, and a lot more besides.

(preposition) Besides tennis, I play soccer and basketball.

clothes / cloths

clothes: something you wear - jeans, shirts, blouses, etc.

Examples: Just a moment, let me change my clothes.

Tommy, get your clothes on!

cloths: pieces of material used for cleaning or other purposes.

Examples: There are some cloths in the closet. Use those to clean the kitchen.

I have a few pieces of cloth that I use.

dead / died

dead: adjective meaning 'not alive'

Examples: Unfortunately, our dog has been dead for a few months.

Don't touch that bird. It's dead.

died: past tense and past participle of the verb 'to die'

Examples: His grandfather died two years ago.

A number of people have died in the accident.

experience / experiment

experience: noun meaning something that a person lives through, i.e. something that someone experiences. – Also used as an uncountable noun meaning 'knowledge gained by doing something'

Examples: (first meaning) His experiences in Germany were rather depressing.

(second meaning) I'm afraid I don't have much sales experience.

experiment: noun meaning something that you do to see the result. Often used when speaking about scientists and their studies.

Examples: They did a number of experiments last week.

Don't worry it's just an experiment. I'm not going to keep my beard.

felt / fell

felt: past tense and past participle of the verb 'to feel'

Examples: I felt better after I had a good dinner.

He hasn't felt this well for a long time.

fell: past tense of the verb 'to fall'

Examples: He fell from a tree and broke his leg.

Unfortunately, I fell down and hurt myself.

female / feminine

female: the sex of a woman or animal

Examples: The female of the species is very aggressive.

The question 'female or male' means 'are you a woman or a man'.

feminine: adjective describing a quality or type of behaviour that is considered typical for a woman

Examples: He's an excellent boss with a feminine intuition.

The house was decorated in a very feminine manner.

its / it's

its: possessive determiner similar to 'my' or 'your'

Examples: Its colour is red.

The dog didn't eat all of its food.

it's: Short form of 'it is' or 'it has'

Examples: (it is) It's difficult to understand him.

(it has) It's been a long time since I had a beer.

last / latest

last: adjective usually meaning 'final'

Examples: I took the last train to Mumbai.

This is the last test of the semester!

latest: adjective meaning 'most recent' or 'new'

Examples: His latest book is excellent.

Have you seen his latest painting?

lay / lie

lay: verb meaning 'to put down flat' - past tense - laid, past participle - laid

Examples: He laid his pencil down and listened to the teacher.

I usually lay my pies on the shelf to cool.

lie: verb meaning 'to be down' - past tense -lay (be careful!), past participle – lain

Examples: The girl lay on the bed asleep.

At the moment, he's lying on the bed.

lose / loose

lose: verb meaning 'to misplace'

Examples: I lost my watch!

Have you ever lost anything valuable?

loose: adjective meaning the opposite of 'tight'

Examples: Your trousers are very loose!

I need to tighten this screw. It's loose.

male / masculine

male: the sex of a man or animal

Examples: The male of the species is very lazy.

The question 'female or male' means 'are you a woman or a man'.

masculine: adjective describing a quality or type of behaviour that is considered typical for a man

Examples: She's a very masculine woman.

His opinions are just too masculine for me.

price / prize

price: noun – what you pay for something.

Examples: The price was very cheap.

What's the price of this book?

prize: noun – an award

Examples: He won a prize as best actor.

Have you ever won a prize in a competition?

principal / principle

principal: adjective meaning 'the most important'.

Examples: The principal reason for my decision was the money.

What are the principal irregular verbs?

principle: a rule (usually in science but also concerning morals)

Examples: It's the first principle of aerodynamics.

He has very loose principles.

quite / quiet

quite: adverb of degree meaning 'very' or 'rather'.

Examples: This test is quite difficult.

He was quite exhausted after the long journey.

quiet: adjective meaning the opposite of loud or noisy

Examples: Could you please be quiet?!

She's a very quiet girl.

sensible / sensitive

sensible: adjective meaning 'having common sense' i.e. 'not stupid'

Examples: I wish you would be more sensible about things.

I'm afraid you aren't being very sensible.

sensitive: adjective meaning 'to feel very deeply' or 'to hurt easily'

Examples: You should be careful with David. He's very sensitive.

Madhu is a very sensitive woman.

shade / shadow

shade: protection from the sun, a dark area outside on a sunny day.

Examples: You should sit in the shade for a while.

It's too hot. I'm going to find some shade.

shadow: the dark area created by something else on a sunny day.

Examples: That tree casts a large shadow.

Have you every noticed your shadow getting longer as it gets later in the day?

some time / sometimes

some time: refers to an indefinite time in the future

Examples: Let's meet for coffee some time.

I don't know when I'll do it - but I will do it some time.

sometimes: adverb of frequency meaning 'occasionally'

Examples: He sometimes works late.

Sometimes, I like eating Chinese food.

Tongue Twister

Definition: A phrase that is designed to be difficult to articulate properly.

A form of verbal play, tongue twisters rely on a sequence of phonemes that are similar but distinct.

See also:

- Alliteration
- Assimilation
- Onomatopoeia
- Reduplicative

  Examples and Observations:

- "We supply wristwatches for witch watchers watching witches Washington wishes watched."

  (James Thurber, Lanterns and Lances. Harper, 1961)

- "Top chopsticks shops stock top chopsticks."

- "Betty Botta bought some butter;
  'But,' said she, 'this butter's bitter!
  If I will put it in my batter,
  It will make my batter bitter.
  But a bit o' better butter
  Will but make my batter better.'
  Then she bought a bit o' butter
  Better than the bitter butter,
  Made her bitter batter better.
  So 'twas better Betty Botta
  Bought a bit o' better butter."

  (Carolyn Wells)

- "What a to-do to die today at a minute or two to two.
  'Tis a thing distinctly hard to say, and harder still to do.
  For they'll beat a tattoo at twenty-to-two,
  A rat-a-tat, tat-a-tat, tat-a-tat, tat-a-tattoo,
  And the dragon will come when he hears the drum,
  At a minute or two to two today, at a minute or two to two."

  (Author unknown)

- "Mary Anning was one of the few women to make a success in palaeontology and one of the fewer still whose success was not linked to that of a palaeontologist spouse (or any spouse: she was single). She made five major fossil discoveries from 1811 to her death in 1847, and many lesser ones.

  "Why then is she best known as the inspiration for the tongue twister 'She sells sea shells by the seashore'?

  "The answer lies in her gender, her poverty, her lack of formal education, her regional accent—as it might even today."

- "[W]e have seen how one sound assimilates to another. As

we pronounce words, our tongue moves toward one point in the mouth, but our nervous system has already prepared itself to fire off another impulse for the next sound. In some cases, the impulses pile up and jumble the articulation, as when we try to repeat a tongue twister like rubber baby buggy bumpers or she sells sea shells by the sea shore."

- "Chester chooses chestnuts, cheddar cheese with chewy chives. He chews them and he chooses them. He chooses them and he chews them. . . . those chestnuts, cheddar cheese and chives in cheery, charming chunks."

Tongue Twisters to Practice Elocution

Young performers face several challenges. For one, they must memorize lines. For another, they must speak loud enough for Grandpa to hear them in the 22nd row. But perhaps the most daunting challenge is learning how to slow down and enunciate.

No vocal warm-up is complete without reciting a few enunciation exercises. With that in mind, I present 26 fundamentally fun tongue twisters. Each one provides an "elocution work out." Take a few for a test drive. Say each line three or four times. But remember, do not worry about speed. Focus on speaking clearly, even if you must over enunciate at first.

A Around the rugged rocks the ragged rascal ran.

B Big black bug bit a big black bear and the big black bear bled black blood.

C Can I cook a proper cup of coffee in a copper coffee pot?

D Don't doubt the doorbell, but differ with the doorknob.

E Eight gray geese in a green field grazing.

F Fine white vinegar with veal.

G Grab the groundhog from the glazed grass.

H High roller, low roller, lower roller.

I Inexplicably mimicking him hiccupping.

J Jingle jungle jangle joker.

K Knit kilts for nasty cold nights.

L Lucy likes light literature.

M Monkeys make monopoly monotonous.

N The Next nest will not necessarily be next to nothing.

O Octopi occupy a porcupine's mind.

P Paras Prangle, the prickly pear picker, picked three perfectly prickly pears.

Q Queen Catherine wakes the cat, and the cat quietly cries.

R Rubber Baby Buggy Bumpers!

S Some shun sunshine. Do you shun sunshine?

T Three thick thistle sticks.

U Unique Mumbai, Unique Mumbai, Unique Mumbai.

V Venti, Grande, Tall - Very Grand Words for Large, Medium, Small.

W Will's wetsuit is round and wet and rough and wide and ready to go on a watery ride.

X Xylophones exist or so existentialists insist.

Y Yoda met a Yeti on the Plains of Serengeti.

Z Zoologists illogically love to read astrology.

Idioms and Expressions

Sooner or later all English students will learn idioms. English uses so many idiomatic expressions that it is truly impossible to learn English without learning at least a few!

Idioms and Expressions with Specific Words

There are certain nouns and verbs that are used in a number of idioms and expressions. These idioms are said to collocate with a specific word.

For example:

put a cork in it

all in a day's work

Idioms and Expressions - 'As ... As'

The following idioms and expressions use the construction 'as ... as'. Each idiom or expression has a definition and two example sentences to help understanding of these common idiomatic expressions with 'as ... as'. Once you have studied these expressions, test your knowledge with this quiz testing idioms and expressions with 'as ... as'.

- **as bad as all that**

Definition: As bad something appears to be

It isn't as bad as all that. You'll be fine tomorrow.

Losing the game isn't as bad as all that.

- **as big as life**

Definition: An exaggerated way to state that someone appeared in a particular place.

There I saw him as big as life!

John came in the room and stood there as big as life.

- **as black as pitch**

Definition: Very dark

I couldn't see a thing in the room because it was as black as pitch.

I can't see a thing. It's as black as pitch. Get a flashlight.

- **as blind as a bat**

Definition: Very bad eyesight

He's as blind as a bat. You can believe what he says.

That ball was in! You're as blind as a bat!

- **as busy as a beaver / as busy as a bee**

Definition: Very busy

I was as busy as a bee over the weekend. I got a lot done.

He's always as busy as a beaver. I wonder if he ever takes a break.

- **as clean as a whistle**

Definition: Very clean

That car is as clean as a whistle now that you've washed it.

I like to keep my desk as clean as a whistle.

- **as clear as crystal**

Definition: Very clear and understandable

Let me be as clear as crystal. Hurry up!

She was as clear as crystal about her intentions.

- **as cool as a cucumber**

Definition: Calm and not nervous

You have to remain as cool as a cucumber to be successful.

I stayed as cool as a cucumber as finished the exercise.

- **as crazy as a loon**

Definition: Very crazy

She's as crazy as a loon. You can't believe a word she says.

I wouldn't worry about his opinion, he's as crazy as a loon.

- **as dead as a doornail**

Definition: dead

That's as dead as a doornail. Forget about it.

The project is as dead as a doornail.

- **as easy as pie**

Definition: Very easy

You'll find the exercise is as easy as pie.

This game is as easy as pie.

- **as far as possible**

Definition: As much as possible

I'll see what I can do as far as possible.

She went as far as possible in trying to get the project approved.

- **as flat as a pancake**

Definition: Very flat

Kansas is as flat as a pancake.

Make sure the table is as a flat as a pancake.

- **as free as a bird**

Definition: Feeling very free and care easy

Our children are away for the weekend so we're as free as a bird.

I used to feel as free as a bird when I was younger.

- **as good as done**

Definition: Almost done

The job is as good as done.

We're almost ready to begin. The cake is as good as done.

- **as happy as a clam**

Definition: Very happy and content

I'm as happy as a clam living in Portland.

She seemed as happy as a clam yesterday.

- **as hard as nails**

Definition: Cruel and very hard

He's as hard as nails with his staff.

Don't work for her. She's as hard as nails.

- **as hungry as a bear**

Definition: Very hungry

Do you have a sandwich? I'm as hungry as a bear.

When we arrived I was as hungry as a bear.

- **as innocent as a lamb**

Definition: Without guilt

There's no way she could have done that. She's as innocent as a lamb.

He's only pretending to be as innocent as a lamb.

- **as mad as a hatter**

Definition: Crazy

Don't believe anything he says. He's as mad as a hatter.

They threw him out of court because he was as mad as a hatter.

- **as old as the hills**

Definition: Very old

My aunt is as old as the hills.

That car is as old as the hills.

- **as plain as day**

Definition: Simple, clear

The facts are as plain as day.

What you need to do is as plain as day.

- **as pleased as punch**

Definition: Very happy with something

He's as pleased as punch with the new boss.

She's as pleased as punch with her new car.

- **as quiet as a mouse**

Definition: Very quiet, shy

She sat in the corner and was as quiet as a mouse at the party.

Can you believe that he was as quiet as a mouse when he was a boy?

- **as right as rain**

Definition: Genuine and true

Yes, that's as a right as rain!

She feels his views are as right as rain.

- **as sick as a dog**

Definition: Very sick

My brother is at home as sick as a dog.

I'm feeling as sick as a dog. I think I need to go home.

- **as sly as a fox**

Definition: Smart and clever

She understood the situation and used it to her advantage because she's as sly as a fox.

Don't trust him because he's as sly as a fox.

- **as soon as possible**

Definition: At the earliest moment possible

Could you reply to my request as soon as possible.

I'll get back to you as soon as possible with the information.

Idioms and Expressions with Verbs

Action verbs are often used in idiomatic expressions. These quizzes focus on verbal idiomatic expressions and use a mix of verbs:

Exercise I

Put each of the following verbs, remembering to conjugate, in the correct gap. Some verbs are used more than once.

drop, kiss, blow, hold, climb, kick, hit, stare, blow, bite

1. Sohan is really trying hard to .... his smoking habit.

2. The stock market crashed so I guess I can .... my profit goodbye.
3. When you get to Japan, make sure to .... me a line and let me know how you are doing.
4. Rohan was .... the wall with impatience.
5. I wish the boss would .... off on his demands.
6. Prem's father .... his lid when he heard about his poor grades.
7. Have you seen Usha's new computer? She must have .... a bundle!
8. The next time Jimmy offends you, just .... him down and he will probably leave you in peace.
9. Don't complain about your boss! You should never .... the hand that feeds you.
10. I'm so depressed. I think that I've truly .... bottom this time.
11. It's time to .... the bullet and start studying for the exam.
12. If you want him to buy you a new car, why don't you .... a hint?

Answers

1. Sohan is really trying hard to kick his smoking habit.
2. The stock market crashed so I guess I can kiss my profit goodbye.
3. When you get to Japan, make sure to drop me a line and let me know how you are doing.
4. Rohan was climbing the wall with impatience.
5. I wish the boss would hold off on his demands.
6. Prem's father blew his lid when he heard about his poor grades.
7. Have you seen Usha's new computer? She must have dropped a bundle!

8. The next time Jimmy offends you, just stare him down and he will probably leave you in peace.
9. Don't complain about your boss! You should never bite the hand that feeds you.
10. I'm so depressed. I think that I've truly hitbottom this time.
11. It's time to bite the bullet and start studying for the exam.
12. If you want him to buy you a new car, why don't you drop a hint?

Definitions

1. Sohan is really trying hard to kick his smoking habit. Kick a habit: stop doing something habitual. Usually used with smoking or drinking
2. The stock market crashed so I guess I can kiss my profit goodbye. Kiss something goodbye: forget about something, except something as not existing anymore in your life
3. When you get to Japan, make sure to drop me a line and let me know how you are doing. Drop a line: get in contact, usually by mail
4. Rohan was climbing the wall waiting for his acceptance letter from the University of Washington. Climb the wall: become extremely impatient
5. I wish the boss would hold off on his demands. Hold off: wait
6. Prem's father blew his lid when he heard about his poor grades. Blow someone's lid: become very angry
7. Have you seen Usha's new computer? She must have dropped a bundle! Drop a bundle: spend a lot of money
8. The next time Jimmy offends you, just stare him down and he will probably leave you in peace. Stare down: confront
9. Don't complain about your boss! You should never bite the hand that feeds you. Bite the hand that feeds you: respond in a negative manner to your employer or provider

10. I'm so depressed. I think that I've truly hit bottom this time. Hit bottom: be very sad or depressed
11. It's time to bite the bullet and start studying for the exam. Bite the bullet: accept a situation
12. If you want him to buy you a new car, why don't you drop a hint? Drop a hint: give a hint to someone

Exercise II

Put each of the following verbs, remembering to conjugate, in the correct gap. Some verbs are used more than once.

crunch, hit, hold, run, feel, keep, bend, give, kill, stand

1. He .... over backwards to help Rahul find a new job.
2. Luckily, Jane .... up for me when the teacher accused me of cheating.
3. I'm afraid I can't make it today. Can I .... you a rain check?
4. If we go shopping on our way home from the lecture, we can .... two birds with one stone.
5. I .... the roof when my son told me he was going to get married at the age of 17!
6. We .... time by playing some video games.
7. I tried to .... abreast of the situation in my home town.
8. Bye! I've got to .... the books because I have a test tomorrow.
9. I was just .... the numbers and I'm afraid we don't have enough money.
10. I have to go to the supermarket. It looks like we are .... out of food.
11. I was .... out of my mind thinking about what could have happened to Sohan.
12. I went over to Nancy's house to .... her company.

Answers

1. He bent over backwards to help Rahul find a new job.
2. Luckily, Jane stood up for me when the teacher accused me of cheating.
3. I'm afraid I can't make it today. Can I give you a rain check?
4. If we go shopping on our way home from the lecture, we can kill two birds with one stone.
5. I hit the roof when my son told me he was going to get married at the age of 17!
6. We killed time by playing some video games.
7. I tried to keep abreast of the situation in my home town.
8. Bye! I've got to hit the books because I have a test tomorrow.
9. I was just crunching the numbers and I'm afraid we don't have enough money.
10. I have to go to the supermarket. It looks like we are running out of food.
11. I was going out of my mind thinking about what could have happened to Sohan.
12. I went over to Nancy's house to keep her company.

Definitions

1. He bent over backwards to help Rahul find a new job. Bend over backwards: make every effort possible
2. Luckily, Jane stood up for me when the teacher accused me of cheating. Stand up for someone: defend someone
3. I'm afraid I can't make it today. Can I give you a rain check? Give a rain check: promise to do something later that you can't do now
4. If we go shopping on our way home from the lecture, we can kill two birds with one stone. Kill two birds with one stone: do two things with one action
5. I hit the roof when my son told me he was going to get married at the age of 17! Hit the roof: become very angry

6. We killed time by playing some video games. Kill time: waste time
7. I tried to keep abreast of the situation in my home town. Keep abreast: to keep up to date, remain informed about
8. Bye! I've got to hit the books because I have a test tomorrow. Hit the books: study
9. I was just crunching the numbers and I'm afraid we don't have enough money. Crunch numbers: calculate finances or statistics
10. I have to go to the supermarket. It looks like we are running out of food. Run out of: have very little of something and needing more, usually used with basic supplies like food, gas, money etc.
11. I was going out of my mind thinking about what could have happened to Sohan. Go out of your mind: become crazy
12. I went over to Nancy's house to keep her company. Keep someone's company: provide friendship to someone.

Idioms and Expressions by Theme

Idioms and expressions often relate to specific themes such as animals.

For example:

kill two birds with one stone

English Clothing Idioms

Try this challenging common English idioms quiz focusing on clothing. Match a line in group A with a line in group B to find the idiom. Next, match the resulting idiom with the definition in group C.

English Idioms Concerning Clothing

Group A

to have ants

to do something at

to hit below

to buckle

to be dressed

to fit like

to lose

to say or do something

to pull something

to tighten

Group B

in your pants

the belt

out of a hat

the drop of a hat

your shirt

to kill

down

off the cuff

your belt

like a glove

Group C

be nervous or restless

lose all or most of your money

get something as if by magic or without any effort

insult someone in an unfair way

say or do something without preparation or impulsively

wear your best, most fashionable clothes

do something without waiting, immediately

live on less money, try to live spending less money

clothing that fits perfectly

give complete attention to doing something

Here are the answers to the English idioms concerning clothing:

1. to have ants in your pants
   - be nervous or restless
2. to do something at the drop of a hat
   - do something without waiting, immediately
3. to hit below the belt
   - insult someone in an unfair way
4. to buckle down
   - give complete attention to doing something
5. to be dressed to kill
   - wear your best, most fashionable clothes
6. to fit like a glove
   - clothing that fits perfectly
7. to lose your shirt
   - lose all or most of your money
8. to say or do something off the cuff
   - say or do something without preparation or impulsively
9. to pull something out of a hat
   - get something as if by magic or without any effort
10. to tighten your belt
    - live on less money, try to live spending less money

English Body Idioms

Try this challenging common English idioms quiz related to the body. Match a line in group A with a line in group B to find the idiom. Next, match the resulting idiom with the definition in group C.

English Idioms: Body

Group A

to happen behind

to have butterflies

to give

to get off

to get under

to be neck

to get something

to pat someone

to be

to stab

to turn

to turn your

Group B

your back

off your chest

your back

on the back

in the back

stomach

the cold shoulder

your back on

your skin

skin-deep

and neck

in your stomach

Group C

treat someone in an unfriendly manner

be equal or nearly equal in a race or contest

tell something important, but difficult to say

say or do something unfair that hurts a friend or someone who trusts you

happen without your knowledge, or when you are absent, secretly

stop criticizing someone

praise someone for a job well done

bother or upset someone

have a feeling of fear or anxiety, be nervous

refuse to help someone in trouble or need

make you feel sick

be only on the surface, superficial

Answers

1. to happen behind your back

   - happen without your knowledge, or when you are absent, secretly

2. to have butterflies in your stomach

   - have a feeling of fear or anxiety, be nervous

3. to give the cold shoulder

   - treat someone in an unfriendly manner

4. to get off your back

   - stop criticizing someone

5. to get under your skin

   - bother or upset someone

6. to be neck and neck

   - be equal or nearly equal in a race or contest

7. to get something off your chest

   - tell something important, but difficult to say

8. to pat someone on the back

   - praise someone for a job well done

9. to be skin-deep

   - be only on the surface, superficial

10. to stab someone in the back

    - say or do something unfair that hurts a friend or someone who trusts you

11. to turn your back on

    - refuse to help someone in trouble or need

12. to turn your stomach

    - make you feel sick

English Animal Idioms

Try this challenging common English idioms quiz featuring animals. Match a line in group A with a line in group B to find the idiom. Next, match the resulting idiom with the definition in group C.

English Idioms: Body

Group A

to bark up

to buy a pig

to be

to cry

to be

to be

to get someone's

to get on

to hold

to horse

to be in

to let the cat

to live high

to look a gift

to make a mountain

to put the cart

to smell

to take the bull

Group B

wolf

an eager beaver

goat

your horses

in a poke

off the hog

out of the bag

a dark horse

around

by the horns

out of a molehill

a cash cow

a rat

the wrong tree

the doghouse

horse in the mouth

your high horse

before the horse

Group C

buy something without knowing if it will be satisfactory

play around in a physical way

have the best of everything

make something that is unimportant seem important

be a candidate little known to the public

be in trouble or disfavour with someone

behave with arrogance

wait, be patient

annoy someone

be a good, and often easy, way to make money

choose the wrong way of doing something

take decisive action

be a person who is always happy to work or do something extra

tell something that is supposed to be a secret

warn of a danger that is not there

do things in the wrong order

be suspicious or someone or something

complain if a gift is not perfect

English Idioms Featuring Animals

Here are the answers to the English idioms featuring animals:

1. to bark up the wrong tree

   - choose the wrong way of doing something

2. to buy a pig in a poke

   - buy something without knowing if it will be satisfactory

3. to be a cash cow

   - be a good, and often easy, way to make money

4. to cry wolf

   - warn of a danger that is not there

5. to be a dark horse

   - be a candidate little known to the public

6. to be an eager beaver

   - be a person who is always happy to work or do something extra

7. to get someone's goat

   - annoy someone

8. to get on your high horse

   - behave with arrogance

9. to hold your horses

   - wait, be patient

10. to horse around

    - play around in a physical way

11. to be in the doghouse

    - be in trouble or disfavour with someone

12. to let the cat out of the bag

    - tell something that is supposed to be a secret

13. to live high off the hog
    - have the best of everything
14. to look a gift horse in the mouth
    - complain if a gift is not perfect
15. to make a mountain out of a molehill
    - make something that is unimportant seem important
16. to put the cart before the horse
    - do things in the wrong order
17. to smell a rat
    - be suspicious or somone or something
18. to take the bull by the horns
    - take decisive action

CHAPTER 7

Improving Grammar

Uses of the Verb To Have

The verb to have is used in a number of different ways in English. Here are the main uses of the verb to have for reference, self-study and in-class use.

To Have – Main Verb

To have is used as a main verb to indicate possession of objects, characteristics, relationships or other qualities.

Examples:

He has three books by Hemingway.

Sanjay has a sister in France.

Firoz has a lot of free time these days.

Have Got

Have got is also used, especially in British English, to indicate possession of objects, characteristics, relationships or other qualities.

Examples:

He's got some friends in Wales.

He's got red hair and freckles.

Ashok has got three cousins.

To Have – Main Verb

To have is also used as a main verb to express a number of actions including:

have a bath, wash, shower, etc.

have breakfast, lunch, dinner

have fun

have time available

have questions

have a party

have a walk, hike, ride, etc.

have a discussion, fight, argument etc.

Examples:

Ekta is having a bath at the moment.

We're going to have a party next week.

She usually has breakfast at seven o'clock.

To Have – Auxiliary Verb

Have is also used as an auxiliary verb in the perfect tenses. Remember that the auxiliary verb takes the conjugation in English, so the verb have will change depending on the tense. Here is a quick review of the tenses that use have as an auxiliary verb:

Present Perfect: He has been to Mumbai twice.

Present Perfect Continuous: They have been waiting for over an hour.

Past Perfect: He had already eaten when she arrived.

Past Perfect Continuous: Jane had been working for two hours when he telephoned.

Future Perfect: They will have been gone for four hours by two o'clock.

Future Perfect Continuous: Mahi will have been playing the piano for two hours by the time he finishes.

To Have To Do – Modal Form

To have to do something expresses the idea that an action or routine is required of someone. We use to have to do something to speak about our responsibilities in life. This form can have the same meaning as 'must', but is generally preferred when speaking about responsibilities. 'Must' is generally used to speak about strong personal obligation (For example: I must talk to Paras. It's important!) Will have to do something is used to speak about future obligations, and had to do something is used to speak about past obligations. The negative form don't / didn't have to do something refers to an action which is not required of someone, but possible nonetheless. 'Mustn't', on the other hand, refers to something that is prohibited.

Present Examples:

Dinesh has to get up early every day.

They have to work hard on Saturdays.

She doesn't have to go to work on Saturdays. (It's possible, but not necessary)

Past Examples:

They had to leave early to catch the flight.

Jennifer had to explain the situation to Paras.

I didn't have to go to the meeting in Delhi. (I could have gone, but it wasn't necessary)

Future Examples:

He will have to get up early tomorrow.

Jyoti will have to decide whether she wants to marry him or not.

They won't have to purchase any additional materials. (They can, but it's not required.)

To Have Something Happen / Happening - Experiences -- Have + object(s) + base form of verb / -ing form

This form is used to speak about experiences that have happened, or experience in general.

Examples:

We have people visit us all the time.

Sherry had her children playing in the garden.

To Have Something Done - Arrangements - Have + object(s) + past participle

This form is used to speak about something that you arrange to have done for you. This form is also known as the causative 'have' because it expresses something which someone else causes to happen.

Examples:

She had them delivered to her home.

We had Jay promoted to director.

English Prepositions

The following list contains the key English prepositions for English language learners. There are more than 150 English prepositions in English. However, this list contains the most commonly used and serves as an excellent starting English prepositions list for most learners and classes. These English prepositions are divided into one word, two word prepositions and three word prepositions. The two word and three word English prepositions are also known as prepositional phrases.

One Word Prepositions

about	above	across
after	against	along
among	around	as
at	before	behind

below	beneath	beside
between	beyond	by
despite	down	during
except	for	from
in	including	inside
into	like	near
next	of	off
on	onto	opposite
out	outside	over
past	through	to
toward	towards	under
until	up	upon
with	without	

Two Word Prepositions

according to	ahead of	aside from
because of	close to	due to
except for	far from	inside of
instead of	near to	next to
out from	out of	outside of
regardless of		

Three Word Prepositions

as far as	as well as	by means of
in accordance with	in addition to	in case of
in front of	in place of	in spite of
on account of	on behalf of	on top of
with regard to		

Adjective Placement

When using more than one adjective to describe a noun place the adjectives in the following order before the noun.

Note: We usually use no more than three adjectives preceding a noun.

1. Opinion

   Example: an interesting book, a boring lecture

2. Dimension

   Example: a big apple, a thin wallet

3. Age

   Example: a new car, a modern building, an ancient ruin

4. Shape

   Example: a square box, an oval mask, a round ball

5. Colour

   Example: a pink hat, a blue book, a black coat

6. Origin

   Example: some Italian shoes, a Canadian town, an American car

7. Material

   Example: a wooden box, a woollen sweater, a plastic toy

Here are some examples of nouns modified with three adjectives in the correct order based on the list above. Notice that the adjectives are not separated by commas.

- A wonderful old Italian clock. (opinion - age - origin)
- A big square blue box. (dimension - shape - colour)
- A disgusting pink plastic ornament. (opinion - colour - material)
- Some slim new French trousers. (dimension - age - origin)

Verb Formation Chart

The following chart shows the positive, negative and question forms of the main tenses in English with a brief description of each tense's usage. Please note that for a better understanding of the tense forms you should follow the links to pages focusing on the specific tense. This chart is principally for comparison purposes. You may also find the visual guide to tenses useful for help in understanding tense usage.

TENSE Simple Past

FORMS:

She went to Paris last week.

They didn't (did not) drive to work.

Where did she get that hat?

USES:

Actions happening at a defined moment in the past.

TENSE Simple Future

FORMS:

I'll (will) meet you at the airport tomorrow.

He won't (will not) be able to come.

Will they visit us soon?

USES:

Decisions made at the moment about the future, future predictions, future promises.

TENSE Present Continuous

FORMS:

He's (is) working at the moment.

They aren't (are not) coming this evening.

What are you doing?

USES:

Actions happening at the present moment. Near future intention and scheduling.

TENSE Past Continuous

FORMS:

I was watching TV when you called.

He wasn't (was not) working when she arrived.

What were you doing when I called?

USES:

Interrupted past action, action happening at a specific moment in time in the past.

TENSE Future Continuous

FORMS:

I'll (will) be cooking dinner when you arrive.

They won't (will not) be living in Paris this time next year.

What will you be doing next week at this time?

USES:

Future action at a specific moment in the future.

TENSE Future with Going to

FORMS:

He's (is) going to fly to Boston next week.

They're (are) not going to invite the Browns.

Where are you going to stay?

USES:

Future intent or planned action.

TENSE Present Perfect

FORMS:

I've (have) seen Mick three times this week.

She hasn't (has not) been to New York.

How long have you worked at Smith's?

USES:

1. To express an action that was begun in the past and continues into the present.
2. To express an action that happened in the Unspecified past.
3. To express a recent action that has a present effect.

TENSE Past Perfect

FORMS:

I'd (had) already eaten before they came.

She hadn't (had not) been to Rome before that trip.

Had you ever seen such a crazy lady before that?

USES:

To express an action that happens before another action in the past.

TENSE Future Perfect

FORMS:

We'll (will) have lived here for twenty years by 2005.

She won't (will not) have finished her homework by the time we arrive.

How long will you have lived in France by the end of next year?

USES:

To express what will have happened or how long something will have happened up to a certain point in the future. More

TENSE Present Perfect Continuous

FORMS:

She's (has) been waiting for over three hours.

They haven't (have not) been studying for long.

How long have you been working on that problem?

USES:

To express the duration of a continuous activity begun in the past and continuing into the present.

TENSE Past Perfect Continuous

FORMS:

She'd (had) been waiting for three hours when he finally arrived.

I hadn't (had not) been sleeping for long when I heard the doorbell ring.

How long had you been playing tennis when she arrived?

USES:

To express the duration of a continuous activity begun before another activity in the past.

TENSE Future Perfect Continuous

FORMS:

He'll (will) have been sleeping for a few hours by the time we arrive.

She won't (will not) have been working for long by 5 o'clock.

How long will you have been driving by 6 o'clock?

USES:

To express the duration of an activity up to a point of time in the future.

Passive Voice

The passive voice is used when focusing on the person or thing affected by an action.

- The Passive is formed: Passive Subject + To Be + Past Particple The house was built in 1989.
- It is often used in business when the object of the action is more important than those who perform the action.

For Example:

We have produced over 20 different models in the past two years. Changes to: Over 20 different models have been produced in the past two years.

- If the agent is important (the person, company or thing that does the action) , use "by"

For Example:

Tim Wilson wrote "The Flight to Brunnswick" in 1987. Changes to: "The Flight to Brunnswick" was written in 1987 by Tim Wilson.

- Only verbs that take an object can be used in the passive voice.

Passive Voice Structure

Active Passive Time Reference

They make Fords in Cologne. Fords are made in Cologne. Present Simple

Susan is cooking dinner. Dinner is being cooked by Susan Present Continuous

James Joyce wrote "Dubliners". "Dubliners" was written by James Joyces. Past Simple

They were painting the house when I arrived. The house was being painted when I arrived. Past Continuous

They have produced over 20 models in the past two years. Over 20 models have been produced in the past two years. Present Perfect

They are going to build a new factory in Portland. A new factory is going to be built in Portland. Future Intention with Going to

I will finish it tomorrow. It will be finished tomorrow. Future Simple

Transitive and Intransitive Verbs

Transitive and intransitive verbs often cause confusion. Let's begin with a simple definition:

Transitive Verbs

Transitive verbs take direct objects. The vast majority of verbs in English are transitive.

Examples:

I took my books to class.

We played chess last night.

Notice that transitive verbs always take objects. You will always be able to ask a question beginning with 'What' or 'Whom'.

Examples:

I paid the bill last week. – What did you pay?

She studies Russian. – What does she study?

Intransitive Verbs

Intransitive verbs do not take direct objects.

Examples:

Peter's situation improved.

They slept peacefully.

You can recognize that a verb is intransitive because it does not have a passive form.

Examples:

Jack sits in the corner when he reads. NOT The corner is sat when Jack reads.

Paras arrived early. NOT Early was arrived Paras.

Transitive AND Intransitive

Some verbs with multiple meanings are transitive or intransitive depending on their usage. The verb 'run' is a good example. When used in the sense of physical exercise, 'run' is intransitive.

Helen ran every weekend when she was at college.

BUT

'Run' used in the sense of managing a company is transitive.

Jennifer runs TMX Inc.

Possessive Nouns and Possessive Adjectives

The formation of possessive nouns and possessive adjectives is sometimes confusing to students. The reason for this is that many languages commonly use 'of' for this construction.

Examples

The colour of his shirt NOT shirt's colour

The ball of his dog NOT his dog's ball

In everyday English, however, we generally use possessive nouns and possessive adjectives rather than this 'of' form.

Possessive Adjectives

Possessive adjectives are used instead of possessive nouns when the reference is understood. For example:

Tom is a dog lover. He takes his dog Spike everywhere!

In this case, it is clear that 'his' refers to Tom because of the context. Possessive adjectives are always placed in front of the noun they modify. Here is a list of possessive adjectives:

I - my dog

You - your cat

He - his book

She - her car

It - its colour (NOT it's!)

We - our dog

You - your house

They - their farm

Examples:

That's my dog in the picture.

Does your cat like tuna?

He left his book in the car.

That's her car over there.

Its colour is purple!

Our dog is like a member of the family.

Your house isn't far, is it?

Their farm produces pumpkins.

Possessive Nouns

Possessive nouns also modify other nouns to indicate possession.

Examples:

Piyush's motorcycle

The building's structure

etc.

Form the possessive pronoun by placing an apostrophe (') after the noun + s.

Paras -> Piyush's motorcycle

building -> building's structure

When nouns end in 's' it can be difficult to know where to place the 's'. For nouns ending in 's', or to use the possessive with regular plurals, place the apostrophe directly after the 's'. Do not add another 's'.

Parents -> parents' concern for their children

Computers -> computers' manufacturer

Notice that this construction can change the meaning from singular to plural.

Examples:

The cat's favourite food is tuna. (one cat)

The cats' favourite food is tuna. (more than one cat)

Possessive Pronouns

Use possessive pronouns to indicate possession when no noun is used. This is the case when the object of possession is understood from the context.

Examples:

Whose book is that? It's mine. = It's my book.

Is this your pen? No, it's hers. = It's her pen.

In both cases, the possessive pronoun can be substituted for the possessive adjective because the object of possession is understood from the context.

Here is a list of possessive pronouns.

I -- mine

You – yours

He -- his

She – hers

We – ours

You – yours

They – theirs

Is this your car? – No, that one over there is mine.

Whose lunch is this? – It's yours.

Whose house is it? – It's his.

Do you know who this belongs to? – It's hers.

This isn't her car. It's ours

Whose picture is this? – It's yours.

Who do those books belong to? – They're theirs.

Finally, possessive nouns can also be used in the same manner as possessive pronouns.

Examples:

Whose cell phone is that? – It's Varun's.

Who do these computers belong to? – They're our parents'.

Use these resources for more detailed information on individual possessive forms:

Possessive Nouns – For example, John's house, the bicycle's colour, etc.

Possessive Adjectives – For example, our neighbourhood, his niece, etc.

Possessive Pronouns – For example, that is mine, this is hers, etc.

Intensifying Adjectives

When describing physical objects you can use a wide variety of adjectives such as: large, big, tiny, minuscule, small, etc. However, when describing nouns that are not physical (e.g. joy, anger, wealth) you need to pay careful attention to the choice of intensifying adjectives. This feature provides a guide to the use of the most common intensifying adjectives for non-physical nouns.

Once you have studied these expressions, try the intensifying adjectives quiz to test your knowledge.

Absolute / Complete / Total / Utter

Absolute, complete, total and utter are used to express strong feelings, extreme situations, and other events - especially negative experiences.

absolute agony

complete astonishment

total bliss

(an) utter catastrophe

absolute despair

total ecstasy

utter fury

a complete idiot

utter loathing

total madness

Big

Big tends to describe a happening or a type of person. It is not usually used with uncountable nouns.

Happenings

a big decision

a big disappointment

a big improvement

a big mistake

a big surprise

Types of Persons

a big eater

a big dreamer

a big drinker

a big spender

a big talker

Great

Great usually describes nouns which express feelings or qualities.

great admiration

great anger

in great detail

(a) great disappointment

great enjoyment

great excitement

a great failure

great fun

great happiness

great joy

at great length

a great number (of)

great power

great pride

a great quantity (of)

great sensitivity

great skill

great strength

great understanding

great wealth

Large

Large is often used with nouns concerning numbers and measurements. It is not usually used with uncountable nouns.

a large amount

a large number (of)

a large population

a large proportion

a large quantity

a large scale

A collocation is a word pair, in this case adjective and noun, that always goes together. There are no specific rules for these collocations, however, it is important to learn some of the standard collocations. Here is a guide to collocations with deep, heavy, high (low) and strong.

Once you have studied these expressions, try the intensifying adjectives quiz to test your knowledge.

Deep deep depression

deep devotion

a deep feeling

deep pockets

deep sleep

in deep thought

in deep trouble

Heavy

a heavy drinker

heavy rain

a heavy sleeper

a heavy smoker

heavy snow

heavy traffic

High – Low.

Notice that a number of nouns (but not all) which take 'high' also take 'low'.

high - or low - cost

high - or low - density

high - or low - energy

high - or low - esteem

a high - or low - expectation (of)

a high - or low - level (of)

a high - or low - opinion (of someone or something)

high - or low - pressure

a - or low - high price

high quality

high speed

Strong

strong criticism

strong denial

a strong feeling

a strong opinion (about something)

a strong sense (of)

a strong smell

a strong taste

Defining and Non-Defining Relative Clauses

Use relative clauses to provide extra information. This information can either define something (defining clause), or provide unnecessary, but interesting, added information (non-defining clause).

Relative clauses can be introduced by:

- a relative pronoun: who (whom), which, that, whose
- no relative pronoun

- where, why and when instead of a relative pronoun

  You need to consider the following when deciding which relative pronoun to use:

- Is the subject or object or possessive of a relative clause?
- Does it refers to a person or an object?
- Is the relative clause a defining or non-defining relative clause?

Note: Relative clauses are often used in both spoken and written English. There is a tendency to use non-defining relative clauses mostly in written, rather than in spoken, English.

Deciding whether a Clause is Defining Or Non-Defining

Defining Relative Clauses

The information provided in a defining relative clause is crucial in understanding the meaning of the sentence.

Example: The woman who lives in apartment No. 34 has been arrested.

The document that I need has 'important' written at the top.

The purpose of a defining relative clause is to clearly define who or what we are talking about. Without this information, it would be difficult to know who or what is meant.

Example: The house is being renovated.

In this case it is not necessarily clear which house is being renovated.

Non-defining Relative Clauses

Non-defining relative clauses provide interesting additional information which is not essential to understanding the meaning of the sentence.

Example: Mrs. Jacobi, who is very intelligent, lives on the corner.

Correct punctuation is essential in non-defining relative clauses. If the non-defining relative clause occurs in the middle of a sentence, a comma is put before the relative pronoun and at the end of the clause. If the non-defining relative clause occurs at the end of a sentence, a comma is put before the relative pronoun.

Note: In defining relative clauses there are no commas.

Relative Pronouns Used As The Subject of Defining Relative Clauses

Example: Children who (that) play with fire are in great danger of harm.

The man who bought all the books by Hemingway has died.

Generally, who and which are more usual in written English whereas that is more usual in speech when referring to things.

Relative Pronouns Used As The Object of Defining Relative Clauses

Example: That's the boy (ø , that, who, whom) I invited to the party.

There's the house (ø, that, which) I'd like to buy.

Relative Pronouns Used As A Possessive In A Defining Relative Clauses

Example: He's the man whose car was stolen last week.

They were sure to visit the town whose location (OR the location of which) was little known.

Note: It is preferable to use that (not which) after the following words: all, any(thing), every (thing), few, little, many, much, no(thing), none, some(thing), and after superlatives. When using the pronoun to refer to the object, that can be omitted.

Example: It was everything (that) he had ever wanted.

There were only a few (that) really interested him.

Relative Pronouns Used As The Subject of Non-Defining Relative Clauses

Example: Frank Zappa, who was one of the most creative artists in rock 'n roll, came from California.

Olympia, whose name is taken from the Greek, is the capitol of Washington State.

Relative Pronouns Used As The Object of Non-Defining Relative Clauses

Example: Frank invited Janet, who (whom) he had met in Japan, to the party.

Paras brought his favourite antique book, which he had found at a flee market, to show his friends.

Note: That can never be used in non-defining clauses.

Relative Pronouns Used As A Possessive In Non-Defining Relative Clauses

Example: The singer, whose most recent recording has had much success, signing autographs.

The artist, whose name he could not remember, was one of the best he had ever seen.

Notes:

In non-defining relative clauses, which can be used to refer to an entire clause.

Example: He came for the weekend wearing only some shorts and a t-shirt, which was a stupid thing to do.

After numbers and words like many, most, neither, and some, we use of before whom and which in non-defining relative clauses. Example: Many of those people, most of whom enjoyed their experience, spent at least a year abroad. Dozens of people had been invited, most of whom I knew.

The Use Of Where, Why And When -Relative Clauses and Preposition Use

Where, referring to a place, why, referring to a reason, and when, referring to a time, can be used instead of a relative pronoun after a noun.

In defining relative clauses why and when, unlike where can be omitted.

Example: I'd like to know the reason (why) he decided not to come.

February is the month (when) many of my colleagues take skiing holidays.

BUT! She always had wanted to go to a place where she could speak her native tongue.

When, where and why are not omitted in non-defining relative clauses.

Example: I come from the Seattle area, where many successful companies such as Microsoft and Boeing are located, and I often go home during the summer.

He likes shopping between one and three, when most people are at home, because of the relative calm.

Notes:

When speaking, we often omit the relative pronoun.

Whom is formal and most often used when writing.

Relative Clauses and Prepositions

In formal English prepositions can come before the relative pronoun. However, it much more common to place prepositions at the end of the relative clause, especially in informal spoken English.

Example: Phagun Oswal, whom I spoke to by telephone, instructed me to buy 200 shares of WAKO. Formal

The Ritz, which was stayed at in New York, was extremely expensive.

Defining Relative Clauses

Example: The banker to whom I gave my check was quite friendly. – formal

The woman I talked to was very pleasant indeed. – informal

The book which I received for my birthday was excellent. – formal

The car he drove was really fast. – informal

Non-Defining Relative Clauses

Example: The bank manager, to whom he addressed his complaints, was very unhelpful. – formal.

The local branch manager, who I talked to about my problems, was very helpful. – informal

Reflexive Pronouns in English

Reflexive pronouns are used much less often in English than in other languages. This explanation provides an overview to reflexive pronoun use in English with explanations and examples.

English Reflexive Pronouns

I – myself

you – yourself

he – himself

she – herself

it – itself

we – ourselves

you – yourselves

they – themselves

Here is a list of some of the most common reflexive verbs in English:

to enjoy oneself

to hurt oneself

to kill oneself

to market oneself

to convince oneself

to deny oneself

to encourage oneself

to pay oneself

Reflexive pronouns are used in three instances in English.

With Reflexive Verbs

Examples: I enjoyed myself last summer.

He's trying to market himself as a consultant.

Sharon pays herself $5,000 a month.

We encourage ourselves to learn something new every week.

As an Object of a Preposition Referring to Subject

Examples: Rahul bought a motorcycle for himself.

They purchased a round trip ticket to New York for themselves.

We made everything in this room by ourselves.

Jackie took a weekend holiday to be by herself.

To Emphasise Something

Examples: No, I want to finish it myself! (I don't want anyone helping me.)

She insists on talking to the doctor herself. (She didn't want anyone else talking to the doctor.)

Frank tends to eat everything himself. (He doesn't let the other dogs get any food.)

Problem Areas

Many languages such as Italian, French, Spanish, German, and Russian often use verb forms which employ reflexive pronouns. Here are some examples:

alzarsi - Italian / get up

cambiarsi - Italian / change clothes

sich anziehen - German / get dressed

sich erholen - German / get better

se baigner - French / to bathe, swim

se doucher - French / to shower

In English, reflexive verbs are much less common. Sometimes students make the mistake of translating directly from their native language and adding a reflexive pronoun when not necessary.

Examples: I get myself up, shower myself and have breakfast before I leave for work. SHOULD BE I get up, shower and have breakfast before I leave for work.

She becomes herself angry when she doesn't get her way. SHOULD BE She becomes angry when she doesn't get her way.

Differences between Action and Stative Verbs

All verbs in English are classified as either stative or action verbs (also referred to as 'dynamic verbs'). Action verbs describe actions we take (things we do) or things that happen. Stative verbs refer to the way things 'are' - their appearance, state of being, smell, etc. The most important difference between stative and action verbs is that action verbs can be used in continuous tenses and stative verbs can not be used in continuous tenses.

Action Verbs

She's studying math with Rahul at the moment. AND She studies math with Rahul every Friday.

They've been working since seven o'clock this morning. AND They worked for two hours yesterday afternoon.

We'll be having a meeting when you arrive. AND We are going to meet next Friday.

Stative Verbs

The flowers smell lovely. NOT Those flowers are smelling lovely.

She heard him speak in Seattle yesterday afternoon. NOT She was hearing him speak in Seattle yesterday afternoon.

They'll love the concert tomorrow evening. NOT They'll be loving the concert tomorrow evening.

Common Stative Verbs

There are many more action verbs than stative verbs. Here is a list of some the most common stative verbs:

be	hate	like
love	need	belong
believe	cost	get
impress	know	reach
recognize	taste	think
understand		

You may notice that some of these verbs can be used as action verbs with different meanings. For example, the verb 'to think' can either express an opinion, or the process of considering. In the first case, when 'think' expresses an opinion it is stative:

I think she should work harder on her math.

She thinks he is a fantastic singer.

'Think', however, can also express the process of considering something. In this case 'think' is an action verb:

They're thinking about buying a new house.

She's thinking of joining a health club.

Generally, stative verbs fall into four groups:

Verbs Showing Thought or Opinions

know

believe

understand

recognize

Verbs Showing Possession

have

own

belong

possess

Verbs Showing Senses

hear

smell

see

feel

Verbs Showing Emotion

love

hate

want

need

If unsure of whether a verb is an action verb or a stative verb the following question:

Does this verb relate some sort of process or a state?

If it relates a process, then the verb is an action verb. If it relates a state, the verb is a stative verb.

Guide to Future with Will and Going to

The Basics: Future with Will:

There are two basic future tenses used to describe things that happen in the future. Besides these two there are some other future tenses. The first future tense is the future with 'will'. Use the future with will to talk about an event in the future that you have just decided to do, for predictions and for promises.

I think I'll go to that party next week.

The economy will get better soon.

Yes, I will marry you.

The Basics: Future with Going to:

The future with 'going to' is used to express events you have already planned in the future and your intentions for the future. We sometimes also use the present continuous for planned events in the near future.

She's going to attend university and study to become a doctor.

We're going to make the presentation next week.

Future with Will Structure:

Positive

Subject + will + verb

I, You, He, She, We, They will come to the party.

Negative

Subject + will + not (won't) + verb

I, You, He, She, We, They won't have time tomorrow.

Questions

Question word + will + subject + verb

What will he, she, you, we, they do?

Future with Going to Structure:

Positive

Subject + to be + going to + verb

I am going to attend the meeting.

He, She is going to attend the meeting.

You, We, They are going to attend the meeting.

Negative

Subject + to be + not + going to + verb

I'm not going to visit U.K. next year.

He, She isn't going to visit U.K. next year.

You, We, They aren't going to visit U.K. next year.

Questions

(Question word) + to be + subject + going to + verb

Where am I going to stay?

Where is she, he going to stay?

Where are you, we, they going to stay?

Guide to Past Simple and Past Continuous

The Basics: Simple Past:

There are two principal past tenses used to make general statements about the past: The past simple and the past continuous. The two tenses are quite different. Use the past simple to talk about an event which happened at some point in time in the past.

Rahul flew to Paris last week.

Paras visited his friends in Mumbai two months ago.

The Basics: Past Continuous:

The past continuous is usually used to refer to events happening at the same time that something important happened in the past.

They were doing their homework when she arrived.

Jay was studying while Usha was cooking dinner..

The past continuous is also used to express what was happening at a precise moment in the past.

I was attending a lecture at 2.30 yesterday afternoon.

Alice was reading a book at six yesterday evening.

Past Simple Structure:

Positive

Subject + Verb + ed OR Irregular Past Form + Objects

I, You, He, She, We, They -> played golf yesterday afternoon.

I, You, He, She, We, They -> went lunch at noon.

Negative

Subject + did not (didn't) + Verb + Objects

I, You, He, She, We, They -> didn't go on vacation last summer.

Subject + did not (doesn't) + Verb + Objects

Questions

(Why, What, etc.) + did + Subject + Verb + Objects?

Did -> I, you, we, they -> attend the meeting last week?

Past Continuous Structure:

Positive

Subject + conjugate the helping verb "be" + verb + -ing.

I was, You were, He was, She was, We were, You were, They were -> watching TV when I arrived.

Negative

Subject + conjugate the helping verb "be" + not + verb + -ing.

I wasn't, You weren't, He wasn't, She wasn't, We wasn't, You wasn't, They wasn't -> working when he came into the room.

Questions

Question word + conjugate the helping verb 'be' + subject + verb + -ing

What -> were you, they -> doing at seven o'clock?

What -> was I, he, she -> doing at seven o'clock?

Passive Voice

The passive voice is used when focusing on the person or thing affected by an action.

- The Passive is formed: Passive Subject + To Be + Past Particple. The house was built in 1989.

- It is often used in business when the object of the action is more important than those who perform the action.

For Example:

We have produced over 20 different models in the past two years. Changes to: Over 20 different models have been produced in the past two years.

- If the agent is important (the person, company or thing that does the action) , use "by"

  For Example: Tim Wilson wrote "The Flight to Brunnswick" in 1987. Changes to: "The Flight to Brunnswick" was written in 1987 by Tim Wilson.

- Only verbs that take an object can be used in the passive voice.

Passive Voice Structure

Active Passive Time Reference

They make Fords in Cologne. Fords are made in Cologne. Present Simple.

Susan is cooking dinner. Dinner is being cooked by Susan. Present Continuous.

James Joyce wrote "Dubliners". "Dubliners" was written by James Joyces. Past Simple.

They were painting the house when I arrived. The house was being painted when I arrived. Past Continuous.

They have produced over 20 models in the past two years. Over 20 models have been produced in the past two years. Present Perfect.

They are going to build a new factory in Portland. A new factory is going to be built in Portland. Future Intention with Going to.

I will finish it tomorrow. It will be finished tomorrow. Future Simple.

■ ■ ■

Chapter 8

Common Mistakes

Apart from confusing words, English language has several expressions that sound familiar but make a world of difference when used. Carefully read about some such expressions and use them carefully in your conversation.

Has gone to *vs.* Has been to

... has/have gone to ... refers to someone who has gone to a place but has not yet returned.

Examples: He's gone to the bank. He should be back soon.

Where has Tom gone?

... has/have been to ... refers to a place which someone has visited sometime in his life. In other words, "has been to" refers to an experience.

Examples: He's been to London many times.

I've been to Disneyland twice.

Good or Well

Good is an adjective and well is an adverb. Many people, including many native speakers, incorrectly use the adjective form good, rather than the adverb well.

Examples: I did good on the test. INCORRECT! – Correct form: I did well on the test.

She played the game good. INCORRECT! – Correct form: She played the game well.

Use the adjective form good when describing something or someone. In other words, use good when stating how something or someone is.

Examples: She is a good tennis player.

Rahul thinks he is a good listener.

Use the adverb form well when describing how something or someone does something.

Examples: She did extremely well on the exam.

Our parents think we speak English well.

Bring Take Fetch/Get

The use of bring and take is confusing for many students. The choice between bring or take depends on the location of the speaker. If the speaker refers to something that is at her current location, she uses bring. Generally, use bring when something moves from there to here.

Examples: I'm glad you brought me to this shop. It's great!

I'll bring the map with me on the trip.

If the speaker refers to something that has been moved to a different location, she uses take. Generally, use take when something moves from here to there.

Examples: The coach took the boys to football field.

Jack took his laptop with him on his trip.

Fetch/Get

When speaking about going somewhere and getting something and then bringing it back, use get (American English) or fetch (British English).

Examples: Could you get the newspaper?

She fetched her diary and showed him the entry.

Difference between OF and FROM in English

Many English learners have difficulties understanding the difference between of and from in English. This comes from the fact that a number of languages, including romance languages such as Italian and French, as well as German, use the same preposition for both of and from. For example, In Italian the phrase, I am from Milan or I come from Milan can be translated as, Sono di Milano. The possessive use of 'of' in English can also use the preposition 'di' in Italian. For example, the phrase, He's a friend of ours can be translated into Italian as, E un amico di noi.

In other words, the preposition 'di' in Italian corresponds to the use of both from and of in English. This is true in many languages. In English, however, there is a distinct difference between of and from.

This short guide to the differences between of and from in English should help you avoid English usage mistakes in the future.

OF

Of - Possession

Of is mainly used as a possessive. For example:

He's a friend of mine.

The colour of the house is red.

It is important to remember that it is more common to use the possessive 's' or the possessive adjective in English, than to use 'of' - even if 'of' is grammatically correct. Thus, the sentences above would generally be in these forms:

He's my friend.

The house's colour is red.

Common Phrases with 'Of' - All of / Both of

Of is also commonly used with 'all' and 'both' to describe a common trait that many objects share. For example,

All of the students in the class enjoy volleyball.

Both of the assignments are due at the end of the week.

Common Phrases with 'Of' - One of the most ...

Another common phrase with of is 'one of the + superlative form + plural noun + singular verb'. This phrase is commonly used to focus on a specific object that stands our from a group. Notice that although the plural noun is used, the singular phrase takes the singular conjugation of the verb because the subject is 'One of the ...'. For example:

One of the most interesting things about my job is the people I meet.

One of the most difficult subjects for me is math.

FROM

From - Origins

From is generally used to express that something originates from something else, that something comes from somewhere, or some person. For example:

Jack comes from Portland.

This formula derives from the work of Paras Schimmel.

This pearl comes from the South Pacific.

From - To / From - Until

From can also be used with the prepositions 'to' and 'until' to mark the beginning and ending point of time of an action or state. Generally, 'from ... to' is used with past tenses, while 'from ... until' is used when speaking about future actions. However, 'from ... to' can be used in most situations. For example:

I played tennis from two until four in the afternoon yesterday.

We are meeting in New York from Monday until Thursday.

Everyone and Every One

Everyone

Use everyone as a pronoun to mean all the people in a group.

Examples: Do you think everyone will want to come to the party?

She wants everyone to leave comments on her blog.

Every one

Use every one as a noun to indicate each person.

Examples: Every one of the students has a question about the grammar.

My boss told every one of the employees himself.

Everyday and Every Day

Everyday

Use everyday as an adjective to mean 'daily'.

Examples: Paras has an everyday appointment with his boss for briefings.

Susan has an everyday yoga class at five p.m.

Every day

Use every day as a time expression to mean 'each day'.

Examples:

Paras studies Russian every day.

She pratices the piano three hours every day.

Whether / If

Both whether and if are used to introduce a yes/no question:

Examples: He asked me whether I felt well.

We're not sure if they have decided.

The verb discuss generally takes whether rather than if.

Examples: We discussed whether he should be hired.

They discussed whether to invest in the new idea.

After Prepositions

Use only whether after prepositions:

Examples: We talked about whether we should go or not.

I looked into whether he should stay.

Infinitives

Use only whether before infinitives:

Examples: She can't decide whether to buy the house or wait.

He considered whether to give up the position or quit next year.

Formal / Informal

Generally, whether is considered more formal than if.

Examples: Let me know whether you will be able to attend the conference.

The CEO will decide whether this is a risk worth taking.

Enough

Adjective / Adverb + Enough

When enough modifies an adjective or an adverb place enough after the adjective / adverb:

Examples: Do you think he is strong enough to lift that weight?

I think it's warm enough to take a walk without my jacket.

Enough + Noun

When enough modifies a noun, place enough before the noun:

Examples: He has enough money to buy a ticket.

She said there were enough participants to begin the study.

A Little - A Few / Little - Few

A little and little refer to non-count nouns, and is used with the singular form:

Examples: There's little wine left in the bottle.

I've put a little sugar into your coffee.

A few and few refer to count nouns, and are used with the plural form:

Examples: There are a few students in that classroom.

He says few applicants have presented themselves.

A little and a few convey a positive meaning.

Examples: I've got a little wine left, would you like some?

They've got a few positions open.

Little and few convey a negative meaning.

Examples: He's got little money left.

I have few friends in Kolkata.

A Lot, Lots Of, A Lot Of

These three expressions are used in informal English. They can mean either a great quantity of or a large number of and can be rather confusing at times. Here are the general rules for their use.

A Lot Of / Lots Of

These two expressions both mean a great deal of or several. They are used before a count or non-count noun. These two expressions tend to be used in informal English.

Examples: We need a lot of people for this game.

She likes lots of jam on her toast.

A Lot

Use a lot at the end of a sentence as an adverb. A lot is NOT followed by a noun. The meaning is the same as a great deal.

Examples: I enjoy swimming a lot.

Madhu seems to travel a lot.

Female – Feminine / Male – Masculine

Female / Male

Use female or male when referring to the sex of people, plants and animals.

Examples: The female bear can be ferocious when defending its cubs.

Are you female or male?

Feminine / Masculine

Use feminine or masculine when referring to a characteristic that you feel is representative of the male or female of the species.

Examples: Some people feel that he is rather feminine.

The decorating was very masculine in that house.

Femininity / Masculinity

These are the noun forms and refer to the state of being either feminine or masculine.

Examples: Femininity was viewed as a curse when displayed by males before the twentieth century.

Some wonder if his masculinity is too stressed.

It's *vs.* Its

It's is the contracted form of It is. This form is used in sentences using "they" as the subject of the sentence with the verb "to be" used as either the helping verb (e.g. It's going ..., It's raining ...) or the principal verb of the sentence.

Examples: It's difficult to find work these days.

It's going to rain soon.

Its is the possessive pronoun form. This form is used to express that "it" has a specific quality, or that something belongs to "it".

Examples: I found its taste to be superb!

Its colour is deep red, almost Burgundy.

Too *vs.* Two vs. To

Too means "also" and is generally used at the end of a sentence. "Too" also indicates too much of a particular quality.

Examples: That car is too expensive for me!

I'd love to come to the party, too.

Two is the written form of the number 2.

Examples: There are two applicants for the job.

She has two cats.

To is generally used as a preposition. It is also used as part of the infinitive form of verbs.

Examples: I gave the book to him.

The verb "to understand" is irregular.

They're *vs.* There vs. Their

They're is the contracted form of They are. This form is used in sentences using "they" as the subject of the sentence with the verb "to be" used as either the helping verb (e.g. They're going ..., They're playing ...) or the principal verb of the sentence.

Examples: They're working hard this week.

They're very interested in helping out.

There is used as an introductory subject is sentences with "There is" and "There are". It is also used as an adverb of place meaning "in that place".

Examples: There are many people in that room.

That's my house over there.

Their is the possessive pronoun form. This form is used to express that "they" have a specific quality, or that something belongs to "them".

Examples: Their house is in Los Angeles.

He liked their looks!

You're *vs.* Your

You're is the contracted form of You are. This form is used in sentences using "you" as the subject of the sentence with the verb "to be" used as either the helping verb (e.g. You're going ..., You're watching ...) or the principal verb of the sentence.

Examples: You're going to have a great time!

You're much better at tennis than Jim.

Your is the possessive pronoun form. This form is used to express that something belongs to "you".

Examples: Your wife is such a kind woman.

I think your skills are outstanding.

Confusing Words

There are a number of confusing word pairs in English.

Here are some examples of some commonly confused word pairs:

effect *vs.* affect

loose *vs.* lose

Since *vs.* For with Present Perfect

Since is used with the present perfect to express that something has happened since a point in time.

Examples: I've lived here since 1999.

She's been working hard since two this afternoon.

For is used with the present perfect to express that something has happened for a period of time.

Examples: I've worked at this job for 10 years.

Peter's been playing tennis for two hours.

Have *vs.* Of

Of is used instead of have in conditional forms due to pronunciation (e.g. I would of visited New York if I had had the time.). "Of" is a preposition whereas "have" is an auxiliary verb used in conditional forms.

Examples: He might have left early on vacation.

She would have attended if you had asked her to come.

Has gone to *vs.* Has been to

... has/have gone to ... refers to someone who has gone to a place but has not yet returned.

Examples: He's gone to the bank. He should be back soon.

Where has Tom gone?

... has/have been to ... refers to a place which someone has visited sometime in his life. In other words, "has been to" refers to an experience.

Examples: He's been to London many times.

I've been to Disneyland twice.

Then *vs.* Than

Then is used as a time expression.

Examples: I'll see you then.

I'll be at the party. We can speak then.

Note: It is not used in the form "different than" which is used for comparisons.

Than is used for comparisons.

Examples: He's lived here longer than I have.

His skills are very different than mine.

Double Negatives

When using the negative form of a verb (e.g. He isn't working ..., They aren't going to ...) do not use a negative quantifier such as nobody, nowhere, etc.

Examples: They aren't going anywhere special. NOT They aren't going nowhere special.

She hasn't spoken to anyone yet. NOT She hasn't spoken to nobody yet.

So ... I

So + Auxiliary Verb + Subject

Use "so ... I" in a positive sense to show that we feel the same way as another person, or have performed the same action. Change the auxiliary verb related to the original statement. The form is usually used in the first person singular, however, other forms are also possible.

Examples: He flew to Geneva last summer. - So did she.

I'd love to visit Poland some day. – So would I.

I'm meeting a colleague tomorrow. – So am I.

Neither ... I

Neither + Auxiliary Verb + Subject

Use "neither ... I" in a negative sense to show that we feel the same way as another person, or have performed the same action. Change the auxiliary verb related to the original statement. The form is usually used in the first person singular, however, other forms are also possible.

Examples: I haven't had a promotion for a long time. – Neither have I.

They weren't sure they had the resources to complete the job. – Neither were we.

She won't be able to attend the conference. – Neither will I.

'Such' and 'So'

Structures using 'such' and 'so' are similar in meaning, but different in construction. The main difference between the two structures is that 'such' takes a noun phrase, whereas 'so' takes an adjective.

'Such ... that'

'Such ... that' takes a noun or modified noun in a noun phrase.

'That' can be used following the noun phrase but is not required.

such + adjective + noun + (that)

Examples: The recording was such a disappointment that I didn't buy any more from that artist.

It was such an expensive car that the didn't buy it.

'So ... that'

'So ... that' takes an adjective. 'That' can be used following the noun phrase but is not required.

So + adjective + (that)

Examples: The game was so fascinating (that) he played for hours.

Our vacation apartment was so luxurious (that) we didn't want to leave.

'So' for Results

'So' can also be used to express a result. In this case 'so' is followed by a full clause:

Examples: I had a lot of time so I visited the museum.

She wasn't happy in her current position so she looked for a new job.

Both ... and

Subjects connected by 'both ... and' take the a plural conjugation.

Examples: Both Alice and Janice attended USC.

Both Jay and Paras are attending the conference in New York this weekend.

Either ... or

'Either ... or' is used in sentences in a positive sense meaning "one or the other, this or that, he or she, etc." Verb conjugation depends on the subject (singular or plural) closest to the conjugated verb.

Examples: Either Paras or the girls need to attend the course. (second subject plural)

Either Jay or Meera is going to visit next weekend. (second subject singular)

Neither ... nor

'Neither ... nor' is used in sentences in a negative sense meaning "not this one nor the other, not this nor that, not he nor she, etc.". Verb conjugation depends on the subject (singular or plural) closest to the conjugated verb.

Examples: Neither Firoz nor Lilly lives in Eugene. (second subject singular)

Neither Atul nor my other friends care about their future. (second subject plural)

■■■

Chapter 9

Exercise your Brain

This series of exercises helps you build your basic phrasal verb vocabulary. Choose the correct definition for the phrasal verbs in the second list from the first list.

Exercise 1

List 1

- become successful
- become extinct
- begin to like a person or thing
- become involved in
- be careful to avoid
- become popular
- be ready to hear
- become accustomed to
- become an adult
- become full of
- be found to be

- become less close
- become
- begin by doing something
- become unlit

List 2

- look out for ....
- listen for ....
- get used to ....
- die out ....
- break into ....
- catch on ....
- go out ....
- take to ....
- turn out ....
- turn into ....
- grow up ....
- fill up with ....
- drift apart ....
- take off ....
- start off ....

Answers

- look out for: be careful to avoid
- turn out: be found to be
- listen for: be ready to hear
- turn into: become
- get used to: become accustomed to
- grow up: become an adult
- die out: become extinct
- fill up with: become full of
- break into: become involved in
- drift apart: become less close
- catch on: become popular
- take off: become successful
- go out: become unlit

- start off: begin by doing something
- take to begin: to like a person or thing

Exercise 2

- look out for
- listen for
- get used to
- die out
- break into
- catch on
- go out
- take to
- turn out
- turn into
- grow up
- fill up with
- drift apart
- take off
- start off

Use the correct phrasal verb you have learned to complete the phrase

- It .... to be a beautiful night tonight!
- He finally .... his wife's cooking.
- Unfortunately, they .... until they finally decided to get a divorce.
- He's trying to .... the tourism industry.
- I .... Atul the first time I met him.
- Finally, the lights .... and we had a good night's sleep.
- Make sure to .... the horn's announcement of the principle theme at the beginning of the second movement.
- He .... in Germany, but moved to the US at the age of 18.
- His books .... and he became a very famous author.
- Let's .... by introducing ourselves. My name is Karan.
- If we don't do something now, the birds are going to .... soon.

- When you go to Malaysia, ... the bad restaurants offering cheap food.
- Amit .... a responsible adult.
- He .... unleaded gas and left on his journey.
- As soon as he moved to Germany, his career ....

Answers

- It turned out to be a beautiful night tonight!
- He finally got used to his wife's cooking.
- Unfortunately, they drifted apart until they finally decided to get a divorce.
- He's trying to break into the tourism industry.
- I took to Atul the first time I met him.
- Finally, the lights went out and we had a good night's sleep.
- Make sure to listen for the horn's announcement of the principle theme at the beginning of the second movement.
- He grew up in Germany, but moved to the US at the age of 18.
- His books caught on and he became a very famous author.
- Let's start off by introducing ourselves. My name is Karan.
- If we don't do something now, the birds are going to die out soon.
- When you go to Malaysia, look out for the bad restaurants offering cheap food.
- Amit turned into a responsible adult.
- He filled up with unleaded gas and left on his journey.
- As soon as he moved to Germany, his career took off.

Exercise 3

List 1

- arrive unexpectedly or after a delay

- (manage to) enter
- abandon attempt
- abolish
- approach someone
- accelerate
- avoid punishment for
- accept a difficult job
- accept as second-best
- be broadcast
- all meet together
- be alert to the danger of
- attend an event
- airplane or helicopter leaving the ground
- approach at speed

List 2

- get into ....
- give up ....
- do away with ....
- speed up ....
- take on ....
- settle for ....
- take off ....
- get together ....
- run up to ....
- come up to ....
- turn up ....
- show up for ....

- get away with ....
- watch out for ....
- go out ....

Answers

- give up: abandon attempt
- do away with: abolish
- speed up: accelerate
- take on: accept a difficult job
- settle for: accept as second-best
- take off: airplane or helicopter leaving the ground
- get together: all meet together
- run up: to approach at speed
- come up: to approach someone
- turn up: arrive unexpectedly or after a delay
- show up: for attend an event
- get away with: avoid punishment for
- watch out for: be alert to the danger of
- go out: be broadcast

Exercise 4

Use the correct phrasal verb you have learned to complete the phrase.

- get into
- give up
- do away with
- speed up
- take on
- settle for

- take off
- get together
- run up to
- come up to
- turn up
- show up for
- get away with
- watch out for
- go out
- Our flight was delayed, but we finally .... shortly after midnight.
- He .... cheating on his final exam!
- I'm trying to .... smoking, but it's almost impossible for me.
- Let's .... with Ajay and Mohan soon.
- Unfortunately, I .... late for my meeting and lost the contract.
- Finally, the lights .... and we had a good night's sleep.
- You won't believe who .... the party! Paras Thompsen!
- I'm afraid I had to .... eggs and bacon. I really wanted to have pancakes, but they were out of them.
- He .... the club on recommendation from his friend Amit.
- I .... and past the policeman doing 120 m.p.h.!
- Unfortunately, our school had to .... the music department because of lack of funds.
- Make sure to .... pick-pockets when you go to the market.
- The boy .... the man and returned his wallet.

- Madhu .... me at the party last night and introduced herself.

Answers

- Our flight was delayed, but we finally took off shortly after midnight.
- He got away with cheating on his final exam!
- I'm trying to give up smoking, but it's almost impossible for me.
- Let's get together with Ajay and Mohan soon.
- Unfortunately, I turned up late for my meeting and lost the contract.
- Finally, the lights went out and we had a good night's sleep.
- You won't believe who showed up for the party! Paras Thompson!
- I'm afraid I had to settle for eggs and bacon. I really wanted to have pancakes, but they were out of them.
- He got into the club on recommendation from his friend Amit.
- I sped up and past the policeman doing 120 m.p.h.!
- Unfortunately, our school had to do away with the music department because of lack of funds.
- Make sure to watch out for pick-pockets when you go to the market.
- The boy ran up to the man and returned his wallet.
- Madhu came up to me at the party last night and introduced herself.

Exercise 5

List 1

- stop doing something
- leave (on a journey)

- apologise or regret having said something
- invent a story
- tolerate
- deny
- review
- separate
- begin a new activity
- become angry
- employ
- finish
- criticise
- find by chance

List 2

- come across ....
- make up ....
- tell off ....
- give up ....
- turn down ....
- take back ....
- put up with ....
- blow up ....
- run out ....
- break up ....
- take up ....
- set off ....
- take on ....
- go over ....

Answers

- come across: find by chance
- blow up: become angry
- make up: invent a story
- run out: finish
- tell off: criticise
- break up: separate

- give up: stop doing something
- take up: begin a new activity
- turn down: deny
- set off: leave (on a journey)
- take back: apologise or regret having said something
- take on: employ
- put up with: tolerate
- go over: review

Exercise 6

- come across
- make up
- tell off
- give up
- turn down
- take back
- put up with
- blow up
- run out
- break up
- take up
- set off
- take on
- go over

Use the correct phrasal verb you have learned to complete the phrase.

- If you really want to lose weight, you need to .... eating desserts.
- Let's .... the grammar one more time before the test.
- I was .... an old sweater when I came across this photograph of my high school class.
- Look Amit, I've .... your bad behaviour long enough!
- There is just too much work to be done. We'll have to .... some new employees.
- You don't think I believe that ridiculous story you ...., do you?

- I think you need to .... a new hobby to help you relax.
- When the father saw what had happened he .... and shouted at his son.
- I had to .... her request for a loan. Her credit was just not good enough.
- We .... at six in the morning on our drive to the Grand Canyon.
- Ajay and Rupa .... last week. They just weren't happy together.
- We'd better stop soon. Otherwise, we'll .... of gas.
- I want you to .... every bad word you've said about my brother.
- Unfortunately, I had to .... Bobby because of his poor performance recently.

Answers

- If you really want to lose weight, you need to give up eating desserts.
- Let's go over the grammar one more time before the test.
- I was looking for an old sweater when I came across this photograph of my high schoolclass.
- Look Amit, I've put up with your bad behaviour long enough!
- There is just too much work to be done. We'll have to take on some new employees.
- You don't think I believe that ridiculous story you made up, do you?
- I think you need to take up a new hobby to help you relax.
- When the father saw what had happened he blew up and shouted at his son.

- I had to turn down her request for a loan. Her credit was just not good enough.
- We set off at six in the morning on our drive to the Grand Canyon.
- Ajay and Rupa broke up last week. They just weren't happy together.
- We'd better stop soon. Otherwise, we'll run out of gas.
- I want you to take back every bad word you've said about my brother.
- Unfortunately, I had to tell off Bobby because of his poor performance recently.

■■■

Other Books on
WORD POWER SERIES

1. Idiomatic English (How to Write & Speak It) **(New)**
2. School Essays, Letters, Applications, Paragraphs, and Stories For Higher Secondary Students
3. Effective English Comprehention Read Fast, Understand Better! **(New)**
4. Latest Essays for College & Competitive Examinations **(New)**
5. Dictionary of New Words **(New)**
6. Art of English Conversation Speak English Fluently **(New)**
7. Teach Yourself English Grammar & Composition **(New)**
8. Common & Uncommon Proverbs **(New)**
9. Effective Editing : Help yourself in Becoming a Good Editor
10. Effective English A Boon for Learners **(New)**
11. Essays for Primary Classes
12. Essays for Junior Classes
13. Essays for Senior Classes
14. Dictionary of Synonyms and Antonyms
15. Dictionary of Idioms and Phrases
16. Common Phrases
17. How to Write & Speak Correct English
18. Meaningful Quotes
19. Punctuation Book
20. Top School Essays
21. How to Write Business Letters with CD
22. Everyday Grammar
23. Everyday Conversation

24. Letters for All Occasions
25. School Essays & Letters for Juniors
26. Common Mistakes in English
27. The Power of Writing
28. Learn English in 21 Lessons
29. First English Dictionary
30. Boost Your Spelling Power
31. Self-Help to English Conversation
32. The Art of Effective Communication
33. A Book of Proverbs & Quotations
34. Word Power Made Easy
35. English Grammar Easier Way
36. General English for Competitive Examinations
37. Spoken English
38. School Essays, Letters Writing and Phrases
39. How to Write & Speak Better English
40. Quote Unquote (A Handbook of Famous Quotations)
41. Improve Your Vocabulary
42. Common Errors in English
43. The Art of Effective Letter Writing
44. Synonyms & Antonyms
45. Idioms
46. Business Letters

Lotus PRESS
Unit No. 220, 2nd Floor, 4735/22, Prakash Deep Building,
Ansari Road, Darya Ganj, New Delhi- 110002
Ph.: 9811594448
E-mail : lotuspress1984@gmail.com, www.lotuspress.co.in